"Nothing in our past seemed to
matter anymore, because the USMC
was starting us all over at square one.
When they cut off our hair, they
exposed all of us for exactly what
we were inside. Our immaturity, lack
of discipline and direction was put right
out in the open for everyone, including us,
to see. I rubbed my bald head as I got out
of the barber chair, and instead of
feeling weird, it felt right..."

Photography: Young Will Price photo by Jorge Baca, USMC; Parris Island scenic photos by Carolyn Price; Recruit Barber Shop photos courtesy of Platoon 1082 Yearbook; Parris Island training photos by Grismer; Pugil Stick photo courtesy of United States Marine Corps' Leatherneck Magazine, photo by Timothy L. Paulin, USMC; Barracks photos by Recruit Price; Marine training photos provided by United States Marine Corps; Graduation Day photos by William Price, Sr.; Fleet Marine Force photo by a member of the United States Marine Corps; About the Author photo by Bucky Barnes, USMC.

The Eagle, Globe, and Anchor (EGA) is the official emblem of the United States Marine Corps. The current emblem traces its roots to the designs and ornaments of early Continental Marines as well as British Royal Marines. The present emblem, adopted in 1955, has only a change in the eagle from the EGA of 1868. Before that time many devices, ornaments, and distinguishing marks followed one another as official marks of the Corps. Use of the the Eagle, Globe, and Anchor symbol and other USMC symbols and trademarks in this book does not constitute the approval, endorsement, or authorization of the United States Marine Corps.

First Printing- 2008
Second Printing- 2011

ISBN: 978-1475119596
PRINTED IN THE UNITED STATES OF AMERICA

www.devildogdiary.com

Also by Will Price:
DEVIL DOG DIARY AFGHANISTAN (2012)

DEVIL DOG DIARY

A DAY-BY-DAY ACCOUNT OF
MARINE BASIC TRAINING
WRITTEN BY THE
RECRUIT WHO LIVED IT

GYSGT. WILL PRICE

CONTENTS

THE OATH 6

FORMING 20

PHASE ONE 42

PHASE TWO 76

PHASE THREE 102

THE FLEET 196

GLOSSARY 198

This was me, Will Price, before joining the Marine Corps. My life, just like my hair in this picture, was an undisciplined mess. Both were about to undergo some major changes.

THE OATH

"Do you know where you're going?" my buddy asked me as we drove to the recruiter.

"Yeah," I mumbled nervously, "To see the recruiter."

"You had to wear *that* hat? You couldn't have shaved?"

"Shut up," I told him, only half-jokingly.

The Army recruiter looked to be about 35 years old. He was nice enough, but he seemed a bit disorganized. His shirt had a little coffee stain on the sleeve. He told me that the Army had a lot to offer — guaranteed career training, as well as travel and some adventure. He told me I should forget about the Air Force because I wore glasses, and that exempted me from being a pilot. He said about the Air Force, "You either fly planes or fix 'em, and if you can't fly 'em there are better opportunities in the Army."

He also talked about how, in the Navy, you had to spend long, long periods aboard ship, sometimes up to six months, without ever going ashore. He described the ships as cramped and lonely — not a pretty picture. And the Marines, he said, couldn't guarantee career training in the field of my choice like the Army could.

I listened closely as he talked, slouching in my chair and nervously twisting my baseball cap backwards and forwards on my head. I always did have trouble sitting still. Our talk lasted about 30 minutes. He almost talked me into signing up for the Army right then and there (recruiters are good at that), but I decided to wait at least overnight to think about it.

When we left the recruiting station, I was feeling tired and lazy, so I told my buddy I wanted to forget about the other recruiters. If I was really going to do this, I was going to go Army. I mean, what's the difference? The military is the military, right?

He smiled. "You're going to see the Marine recruiter," he told me, "whether you like it or not."

The minute I saw the Marine recruiter, a Staff Sergeant from Ohio, I knew right away he was different from the Army guy. He radiated confidence. He acted like he owned the world. Two Marines who had just finished basic training happened to be in the recruiting station. They were very enthusiastic, and also bursting with self-confidence. Their uniforms were totally clean and neat, and their posture was ramrod-straight.

I could sense that they were somehow bonded. They were a part of an elite "club," and I could feel myself already wanting to join that club. Up on the wall, I saw pictures of Marine recruits in their "blues" uniforms, along with some letters they had written to the recruiter from boot camp. It was weird, because I kept imagining myself in one of those pictures, and imagining *my* letters on that wall. I suddenly wished I had shaved that morning. I made sure to sit up straight in my chair. We talked for about 45 minutes.

When I asked about career training, I got an answer that really made an impact on me. It upset me and intrigued me at the same time.

"If you want to join the Marines," the recruiter told me, "You have to want to be a Marine first. Career training is secondary. You only *join* the other branches — you *become* a Marine."

As he told me that, I reached up and started to turn my baseball cap around on my head. I got it twisted about half way, then suddenly stopped, and quickly faced it to the front again. Turning it backward suddenly seemed horribly immature and disrespectful.

In that instant, my decision was made. I wanted to be like this guy. He wasn't confused and drifting along through life like me. He was strong, proud and confident. He had something else I couldn't quite put my finger on — some kind of inner power. Whatever it was, I knew it was awesome, and I knew I wanted it. At that moment, I knew I had found my calling.

I was ready to sign up on the spot, but I found out that it isn't that easy. First, I had to pass an intelligence test, and then get a physical. Then I had to pass a strength test. And I had a police record that had to be dealt with. I took a deep breath, and made the necessary appointments.

What police record? When I was 18 and 19 years-old, in my wild college days, I got arrested for doing some immature and stupid things that seemed like fun at the time. Things like vandalizing a mailbox while visiting a friend at his college. I paid it off and the charges were dropped. Sorry Mom, I forgot to tell ya' about that one.

Another time, about six of my buddies and I decided to flip over a girl's car just for fun. The cops didn't seem to think it was so funny. Same result, only it cost me quite a bit more cash. My next encounter with the law was a biggie. I got into a brawl involving five guys that landed me and my two friends in jail for a night, then prison, for a very long weekend. That fight taught me a valuable lesson: Usually, it's not the guy who *starts* the fight who gets arrested... it's the guy who *wins* the fight.

So was I a hardened criminal? Hardly. At the time, however, I was scared about where I was headed. I was scared about what my parents would think of me. I was scared that I was losing my morals, and I had definitely lost my honor. To change, I knew that I would have to begin deep down, within me.

A few weeks after my meeting with the Marine recruiter, I took a military intelligence test, called the ASVAB (Armed Services Vocational Aptitude Battery). The test consists of different sections, including math skills, word knowledge, science, paragraph comprehension, mechanics, and electronics. The test took three hours to complete. A few days later, my results came back — I scored a 92 out of a possible 99.

The next hurdle was the physical. I wasn't worried about that, since I was in pretty good shape (or at least I *thought* I was). Marine applicants all meet at the recruiting station the night before the physical, and then are taken to a hotel for the night. The next morning they go to the nearest MEPS (Military Enlistment Processing Station). The military seems to have an acronym for just about everything. The MEPS performs physicals for all four branches of the military, not just the Marines.

The day before the physical, I showed up at the recruiter's office with a mop of messed-up hair sticking out all over the place, needing a shave, in a wrinkled old T-shirt and ragged shorts with shoelaces flying everywhere. Comparing my appearance to the Marines, I began to realize that if I wasn't *living* in a dream world, I was definitely *dressing* in one. To make things worse, the recruiter gave me a dirty look as I walked in — 20 minutes late.

"You showed up after all," he said.

"Yeah. Sorry, I'm such a mess." His sober expression changed. "Don't worry," he told me, "We'll take care of that soon enough." Then he let out one of his little, 'I know something you don't know' chuckles.

After some hugs and kisses from my family, I was shuttled to a hotel in Brooklyn, where I met a bunch of other guys and girls about to take the plunge. Everyone was very quiet, almost like we were in church. I shared a hotel room with a guy named Ruiz, who was also joining the Marines. We split a six-pack of Heineken and talked a long time about why we were joining, and our goals and aspirations. He seemed a bit confused, and I wondered if he was going to make it. I also wondered if I was going to make it. We went to sleep around midnight. Four hours later, the phone rang.

It was our wake-up call. We were to be showered, shaved and ready for our physicals in one hour. My first taste of military discipline! As I dragged myself out of bed at 4 a.m., I imagined doing it every day, and wondered again what the hell I was getting myself into.

The physical went well. I passed every test, and at the end of the day, I signed up to join the United States Marine Corps. There was only one problem — I still had to deal with my arrest record before I could be sworn in. They told me a clearance would come through in about an hour, and I was a nervous wreck waiting for it to come. I was fidgeting all over the place, pacing around, wondering if I had screwed up my life for good by doing all the stupid crap I had done previously. Two hours later, word still hadn't arrived. Three hours later, I was ready to scream. I couldn't sit still. I never could, but this was even worse.

I was ready to forget the whole thing, when finally, around four hours later, I finally received the necessary clearance. I was ready to take the oath and be sworn in. Me and about 20 other guys and girls filed into a small room with a row of flags at the far end. A man wearing a uniform entered. He blasted the room with a booming, clear voice and said:

"STAND UP STRAIGHT, WITH YOUR FINGERS CURLED, THUMBS TOUCHING THE SEAMS OF YOUR PANTS, AND YOUR FEET AT A 45-DEGREE ANGLE. KEEP YOUR EYES FRONT, AND

DO NOT TALK. THIS IS THE POSITION OF ATTENTION!"

He wasn't there to intimidate us, but he was definitely there to let us know that we were "not in Kansas anymore." Then, another man in uniform came in, someone of higher rank, and, as he recited the military oath of enlistment (which is the same for all the branches) we repeated:

"I, William Price, do hereby acknowledge to have voluntarily enlisted under the conditions prescribed by law, this 24th day of February, 1995, in the United States Marine Corps for a period of four years unless sooner discharged by proper authorities; and I do solemnly swear (or affirm) that I will support and defend the Constitution of the United States against all enemies, both foreign and domestic; that I will bear true faith and allegiance to the same; and that I will obey the orders of the President of the United States and orders of the officers appointed over me, according to regulations and the Uniform Code of Military Justice, so help me God."

It was the first time I had ever sworn to anything. As I heard myself saying the words, I wondered if I was doing the right thing. Then I remembered the inside of that jail cell, and the awesome, indescribable something I had seen in the Marine recruiter. No matter what, I thought, this is more than my last chance, I felt as if it were my destiny. There would be no backing down anymore. Besides, on a practical level, it was too late to change my mind anyway!

SUNDAY, MARCH 12

I had been told to arrive at my local Marine Recruiters station at 6:00 p.m. on Sunday night. From there, I was to be taken to the airport, along with some 11 other guys who were also joining up. My father had moved to Manhattan after my parents got divorced, and he came up to my house in Westchester to see me off. I put on my best pair of worn-out jeans and my favorite Grateful Dead T-shirt, and told my parents I was ready to leave.

"You're wearing *that*?!" my father asked.

"Yeah," I said, "So what?"

"Aren't you at least going to shave?"

"What for?" I answered.

"I think you should," my mother said.

"Don't tell me what to do," I answered defiantly.

It was pretty quiet as we drove with my younger brother, John, to the recruiting station. I was getting more nervous by the second, and as we pulled up to the parking lot I almost changed my mind about the whole thing. We parked, and I walked to the recruiting office like a condemned man walking the last mile. Inside, we were shown a video about the training I'd be getting on Parris Island. About 15 minutes into the video, my buddy Kirk walked in. I was glad to see him. He asked me to come outside for a minute, so he could tell me something.

"Well, this is it," he said.

"Yeah," I said nervously. "Am I doing the right thing?"

"Rightest thing you've ever done," he told me. "You may not understand that now, but you will. They're going to help you make some changes in your life."

"They're not going to change me," I said cockily. "I think it'll be easy."

He laughed out loud. "Well, we'll see. Listen, I know you're having second thoughts. You may not believe this, but there will come a time when you can't imagine what your life would have been like if you hadn't become a Marine."

"You really think so?"

"I know so."

He handed me a letter. "Here. I want you to read this on the bus as you go to Parris Island."

"Yes sir," I told him sarcastically.

"Good luck, buddy! I'll see you in a few months. Good-bye to Billy Price."

"Why are you saying it like that?"

"Because the next time I see you, you'll be a different person."

"Yeah, maybe," I said nervously, "Thanks for everything," I said tentatively. I wasn't sure if I should thank him or not. Was I really doing this? I got out of the car and walked back into the recruiting station. My parents and brother left, and before I knew it I was on a bus headed for the airport, along with 11 other Marine recruits and a few recruits from other branches.

MONDAY, MARCH 13

Altogether, our "Marine" group was 12 strong. It's funny because even though we were still the same sloppy kids on the outside, deep down I knew otherwise. At the MEPS, myself and another recruit were chosen to be in charge of our "dirty dozen." This responsibility may not sound like very much, but I felt like out of the thousands of others at the airport, I was leading the twelve of us on a mission. Our objective, if we chose to accept it; was to arrive safely at Parris Island.

The connecting flight to Atlanta was scheduled to take off at 5:15 p.m., and from there we would connect to Charleston, South Carolina, and land at 10:35 p.m. After that would come the bus ride to Parris Island, and 12 weeks of basic training. I'd been real nervous all day. I took three or four catnaps during the day, but that didn't quite cut it. I was still very tired and apprehensive about what was in store for me.

On the flight to Atlanta, I managed to sleep restlessly for about an hour. I decided to keep a journal, to record the experiences I would be going through on Parris Island.

Everything I've recorded up to this point, I wrote on the plane to Atlanta — but from this point on, I will be writing everything down, day-by-day, as it happens.

When we landed in Atlanta, I called my mother, Carolyn. It was good to talk to her, and let her know I was all right. From the beginning, she wasn't too thrilled with the idea of her baby boy joining the Marines, but I eventually convinced her that it was the best thing for me. Now if I could only convince myself.

On the flight to Charleston, almost everyone was joking and carrying on. Some were loud, some were quiet, and some were both — like me. A few guys were whistling the Marines' Hymn. It was sort of like a party atmosphere, until the plane landed. Suddenly, we all

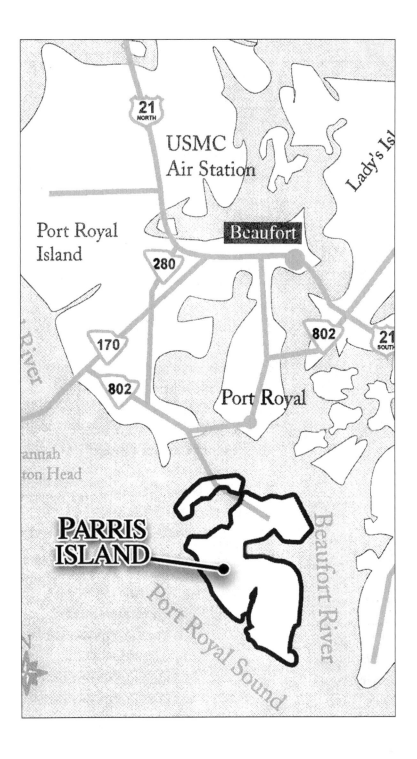

became very serious, almost like funeral silence. It was then, while departing the plane, that we saw two Marines in uniform, waiting for us at the end of the exit ramp. The mood quickly changed. As we headed down the tunnel, everyone turned deadly serious. The reality that we were now the property of the United States Marine Corps quickly sank in. Their booming voices spat out commands, leaving no room for misunderstanding.

"SIT DOWN AND BE QUIET," they told us. "KEEP YOUR FEET ON THE GROUND IN FRONT OF YOU, AT A 45-DEGREE ANGLE."

The Marines are big on 45-degree angles. They told us to get rid of all our "contraband" (forbidden personal items), so we emptied our pockets of pens, condoms, candy, etc. As I stood there silently, I looked at the Marines. They all had that awesome, "certain something," I had seen in my recruiter. Their pants were neatly pressed, their uniforms absolutely clean. They were immaculately groomed. They were confident, proud, full of discipline — all qualities I lacked. I was totally undisciplined and without direction. I had no self-confidence. My hair was a mess. I needed a shave. I wondered what the hell I was doing, and how I could ever make it as a Marine. I was scared.

We were finally led out of the airport just before midnight, and the first thing that hit me about South Carolina was the foul smell of the marshland air in the morning, an odd mixture of sewage and sulfur. They marched us into a big old coach bus that was waiting for us. We piled on — nervous, tired, excited — and sat down in dead silence.

Even as tired as I was, I thought I'd never be able to get any sleep, but I was wrong. I think they drove the bus around the airport a few extra times just to make the trip longer and make us more exhausted than ever, so that we wouldn't have the strength to resist the ordeal we were about to undergo. My stomach was one big knot as I opened the letter my buddy gave me.

Dear Will,

Archimedes, the inventor of the lever, once said, "Give me a lever large enough... and I will *move the world*." Will, the Marines are going to be your "lever," and if you put your mind to it, you can, and *will*, move the world.You're about to undergo an incredible transformation.

All reminders of your past will soon be taken away – all that will remain is your personality. And soon, even that may change. Scary? You'd better believe it. But it's necessary. There's no other way to break you of years of bad habits. You may think basic training is going to destroy your individuality — but trust me, the end result will be that you are going to become *more* of an individual than ever before.

You've got an awful lot to give, buddy. You just need something to give it to. And that something is the Marines. Don't ever wish you hadn't joined up pal, because we've both come to realize that becoming a Marine is something you have to do. Not everyone understands why. Some people may never understand why. They'll say, "Come on Will, are you crazy? What do you think you're really going to accomplish by joining the Marines?"

And when they do, you'll proudly reply, "I didn't *join* the Marines, I *became* a Marine. What am I going to accomplish? I'm going to *move the world.*"

Just a short while to go until your great adventure begins – the greatest adventure a man can have – the adventure of self-discovery. The unforgettable experience of coming face-to-face with yourself, and learning who you are. Remember, when you step off this bus, it all begins. You end a life chosen for you by others, and begin a life of your own choosing. Your destiny is finally in your own hands. Make the most of it.

Not everyone understands why – but I do. And more importantly, YOU do. I can't wait to see the finished product – a proud, mature, self-confident man – a MARINE.

Good luck buddy — MOVE THE WORLD!

I felt a lot better after reading this letter — it was like he read my mind and knew what I needed to hear. I was still nervous. I was still scared – but I knew I was doing the right thing. Sitting around my house watching MTV sure as hell wasn't going to get me anywhere. He was right – this was something I had to do.

I shut my eyes and drifted off to sleep.

This is the only road on — or off — Recruit Depot Parris Island. The bus driver told us, "Good luck! Get your last laughs out now, then straighten up and brace yourselves!"

Once we arrived on Parris Island, a Drill Instructor boarded the bus, and the reality that we were now the property of the United States Marine Corps quickly sank in.

TURN
THE
PAGE,
RECRUIT

The yellow footprints, where nearly 40,000 recruits a year take their first step towards becoming Marines. Male recruits living west of the Mississippi River train at Marine Corps Recruiting Depot San Diego, California. Male recruits living east of the Mississippi River, and all female recruits, regardless of location, train at MCRD Parris Island, South Carolina.

FORMING

TUESDAY, MARCH 14

When I woke up from my brief nap on the bus, I was only a few miles away from boot camp. I saw a sign that read: PARRIS ISLAND 3 MILES, and the butterflies in my stomach started to build up again. Soon, there it was — the big red sign I had seen in pictures. Now, it was right in front of my face: MARINE CORPS RECRUIT DEPOT, PARRIS ISLAND. We drove down the main road – the *only* road – through the swamps and woods, and finally the bus slowed. It was now 2:00 in the morning, and pitch black outside. After passing a guard post, the driver slowed the bus and spoke over her shoulder to us.

"Good luck! Get your last laughs out now, then straighten up and brace yourselves!"

We drove on. It seemed like forever until we saw any kind of buildings. Then, out the window, I could see a dark figure. Judging by his posture, it could only be a Marine. He was moving quickly toward the bus. He looked meaner than life. He boarded the bus and screamed at us, "DO WHAT I SAY, AND DO IT QUICKLY! NOW GET OFF OF MY BUS! MOVE! MOVE! MOVE!"

We ran off the bus and hit the pavement. I started to look around, and another Marine came up to me and screamed in my ear, "GET ON THOSE YELLOW FOOTPRINTS! EYES FRONT! YOU! QUIT LOOKING AROUND!"

There were a series of yellow footprints, painted on the road, showing the 45 degree angle we were supposed to keep our feet in – the "position of attention." It was hard for me to believe that reality had actually brought me here. I thought to myself, "Is this really happening? Am I really here? Did I really do this? Could it be I'm just dreaming?"

"RECRUIT!" a Marine screamed in my ear, "GET YOUR FEET ON THOSE FOOTPRINTS!" My heart started pounding. I realized it was all as real as real can be. Next, we were marched into a building

next to the road with the yellow footprints. A huge metal sign over the doors read, "THROUGH THESE PORTALS PASS PROSPECTS FOR AMERICA'S FINEST FIGHTING FORCE – UNITED STATES MARINES." I thought... is that *me?*

Inside the building was a room full of desks. We were told to sit down. After I did, I was screamed at some more, and told to write my Platoon number — 1082 — on the back of my hand with a big black magic marker. I felt like I was being branded. In a way, I was. We were given a bunch of forms, and told to fill them out. I sat there writing furiously, answering every conceivable question about myself: personal information, medical history, tax information, life insurance, and more. It seemed endless. I thought, "After I'm done, they'll know every last friggin' detail about Billy Price's sorry life."

A few times, they told me to put my head down on the desk while I waited for another set of forms. Each time I did, I soon fell asleep — and was abruptly awakened by a Marine screaming in my face.

"RECRUIT! WAKE UP! EYES OPEN!"

Finally, after about 3 1/2 hours, we finished the paperwork. Then they lined us up again, handed each of us a fistful of toilet paper, and headed us toward an adjoining room. As I got closer, I heard the distinct sound of electric clippers buzzing away.

I glanced ahead to see what was going on, and was instantly attacked.

"KEEP YOUR EYES STRAIGHT AHEAD! STAY IN LINE!"

"Okay, all right," I responded. The Marine who told me to keep my eyes straight exploded.

"RECRUIT, FROM NOW ON THE FIRST WORD OUT OF YOUR MOUTH AND THE LAST WORD OUT OF YOUR MOUTH IS TO BE **SIR**. IS THAT UNDERSTOOD?"

"Sir, yes sir," I mumbled nervously.

"WHAT?"

"Sir, yes sir!" I tried to shout.

"I STILL CAN'T HEAR YOU!" the Marine screamed at me louder than anyone ever had in my whole life, even my mother. Up to this point in my life, I had thought I was so hard, such a tough guy. Petrified, I roared, "SIR, YES SIR!" at the top of my lungs. "What is happening to me?" I kept thinking.

As the line advanced, I rounded a corner into the recruit barbershop. There were three barber chairs in it — all facing away from the large mirror covering the wall. I didn't dare look to see the recruit who was getting his hair cut, but out of the corner of my eye I saw that the floor was covered with hair. The guy in front of me was soon ushered into the chair, and I was told to stand directly in front of him. The barber was an old-timer who moved in a blur of motion as he threw a red cloth around each recruit's neck and grabbed his electric clipper.

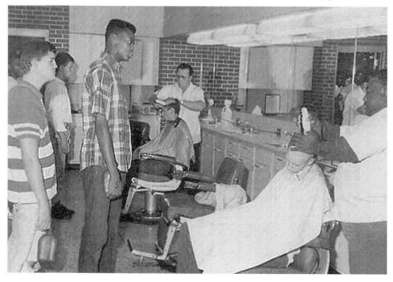

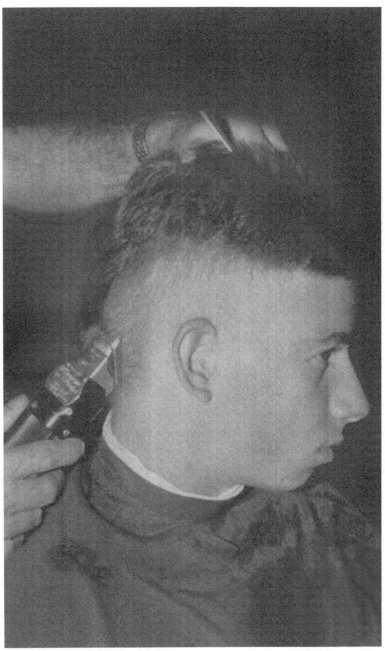

Here I am getting my first boot camp haircut! During the thirty painful seconds it took to get, all I kept thinking was, "What have I gotten myself into?"

"Oh God," I thought as I watched what was being done to his mop of hair. I had expected a military haircut, but nothing like this. They were shaving us totally bald! I couldn't believe how fast the barber was going. With each pass of the razor, he shaved a path in the guy's head that went all the way down to his scalp. In about 30 seconds or less, the guy was completely bald. The last few locks of his hair floated down and landed on the floor, then the cloth around his neck was unsnapped and the barber yelled, "NEXT!"

I couldn't believe this was going to be done to me. I wanted to run and jump back on the bus, but I was so tired, I could barely keep my eyes open – which, I guess, is exactly how they planned it. I hesitated a moment, then a Marine charged up to me and screamed in my ear.

"GET IN THE CHAIR, RECRUIT!"

"SIR, YES, SIR!" I screamed as loud as I could – I was learning... or so I thought.

"NOW! NOW! NOW!" was the deafening response.

I glanced in the mirror and took a last look at the old me, then jumped in the chair. Before I knew it the red cloth was around my neck, and the barber was going to work on me, shaving my head. Seconds ago I had watched that other guy's hair falling to the floor. Now hair was still falling to the floor – but it was all mine.

I discovered why the other guys were all wincing – man, did that razor cut deep and hard! I squeezed the fist-full of toilet paper I had been given as the barber shaved the side of my head. He grabbed my head and pushed it forward, then buzzed off the back and other side, then plowed through the top. Thirty seconds after it had begun, the fastest and most complete haircut I ever received was over.

I got out of the chair and was told to hold my head over a large garbage can and brush it off with the toilet paper. My bald head felt like someone else's as I brushed it off and watched little bristles of hair fall into the can. When I was done, I whirled around to sneak a quick glimpse at myself. When I saw my reflection, I was shocked. I didn't recognize myself. I thought I was looking at someone else, but I wasn't – it was me. At least, I *think* it was.

Next, I was moved along into a long, narrow room. My civilian clothes – my favorite Grateful Dead T-shirt, ragged jeans and underwear – were taken away. I was issued my first uniform, boots, hat – or "cover" as it's called – belt, and underwear, or "skivvies." We were told to quickly remove our civilian clothing and put on our uniforms, called "cammies" (short for "camouflage," the pattern covering them). As fast as I could, I tore off my old clothes and put on my new uniform. It felt weird. Wearing cammies for the first time, with my new cover pulled down tight against my bald head, once again I couldn't believe I was actually doing this.

Next, we were herded to a medical facility for testing. They took so much blood out of me, I thought I was going to pass out. After that, we got in another line. As I went through it, two doctors grabbed each of my arms and stuck something that looked like a gun against them, then pulled the trigger and injected me – I have no idea with what. I was ready to drop. I had never been so tired. I was so exhausted, I began to feel like a robot moving through an assembly line. And with each step I took, I lost a little bit more of the old me.

It was now 5:30 in the morning. I had been awake for about 42 hours, minus a couple of hours of short naps. With my new haircut, carrying my extra new uniforms, and my platoon number – 1082 – marked on the back of my hand in magic marker (or "El Marko," as the Marines call it), I shuffled outside. We lined up again, then visited the store, a.k.a., "made a PX call." I'm discovering that the Marines have a unique word or term for nearly everything. Carrying a laundry bag with some 40 pounds of toiletries in it, I marched over to the receiving barracks for the first time. This is where I'd be staying during the rest of what's called "Forming Week." I thought for sure I'd be allowed to sleep now, but I thought wrong.

As a unit, we marched pretty sloppily to the chow hall for some breakfast. I discovered right away that the chow hall is very regimented and strict – especially for new recruits like myself. There was no talking at all unless it was to order food. I was only allowed to drink water from a canteen, because drinking juice is a privilege reserved only for Training Recruits, and at this point I was just a Receiving Recruit. I also realized that even my name had been taken away. From now on, I had no first name – from now on I was simply to be known as a "recruit" with a number on his hand. I began to wonder what I had left.

"STAY MOTIVATED, RECRUIT!" I heard these words of inspiration over and over when I got to bootcamp. Getting administratively processed into the system is a very long and tiring experience.

It was here, in the chow hall, that I first encountered three magical words that make you either want to strangle someone, or, if you take them as they're meant to be received, to thank them. Those three words will forever be embedded in my mind. They are: "STAY MOTIVATED, RECRUIT!"

We headed to another room, where we were checked out for fraudulent enlistment. Everyone was pretty tense. Some recruits broke down – they admitted that they had tried to join up under fraudulent circumstances, and they were taken into another room. Who knows *where* they went, since they didn't come out in the two hours it took to process about 160 of us. I had ridiculous visions of a torture chamber somewhere. Those who remained had their info put into a computer.

By now it was time for lunch. This was served in a bag, and – you guessed it, there's a special name – it was called a "bag nasty." Your typical bag nasty consists of a mystery-meat sandwich, a piece of fruit, a hard-boiled egg and some cookies. A lot of the guys hated them, but I didn't really have any problem chowin' em down.

After lunch, we began learning the basics of marching, cleaning, hygiene and being a Marine Recruit. All in all, it was one long-ass day that I thought would never end. Then we were led back to receiving barracks, and told to lie down in our beds, or "racks." But even in bed, we had to lie down in the position of attention! In a few minutes, we were ordered to "adjust," which meant we could get under the covers and go to sleep. We had been awake for almost 55 straight hours. Finally, the longest three days I ever lived through were over – but I was so tired I almost couldn't sleep.

Imagine, just a few short days before my ordeal began, I was boasting that 12 weeks of Boot Camp wasn't going to change me – but now, in only a few hours, the Marines had squeezed everything I used to be out of me like toothpaste from a tube. And, they were going to keep on squeezing until there was nothing left of the old me. I know now, that I *am* going to change here on Parris Island, and not just a little. I guess that was what I wanted when I joined up, but now that it's actually *happening*, I'm not so sure about it. The Marines are going to make me into a different person. Who that person will be, I don't know. All I know is that I've never been so scared, confused and exhausted before in my whole life!

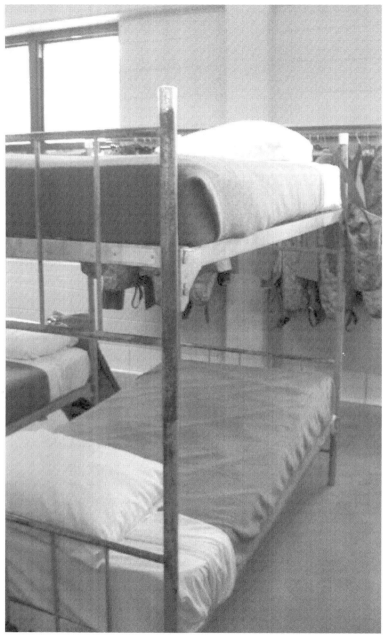

*One of the first things we learned at bootcamp was how to make a military "rack."
The term bed no longer existed for Recruit Price. For the record, these racks could
have been made a lot tighter!*

I fell asleep and dreamed that I was back at home. I heard my Mom in the kitchen making breakfast. I felt such a sense of comfort in this. I thought, "What a nightmare I just had. I was a Marine Recruit somewhere on Parris Island. I sure am glad that's over." When I woke up, I found myself looking up at the bottom of the top bunk. I was confused. I was thinking, "Where the hell am I?" Then it hit me. I reached up to scratch my head, and when I felt my new haircut I remembered where I was. This was definitely *not* the kitchen that good old Carolyn built. I slowly drifted back to sleep.

Recruit Price is a long way from home.

WEDNESDAY, MARCH 15

At 3:00 am sharp – BAM – the lights went on. It was a real shock to my system. When the Drill Instructors started yelling, I suddenly remembered, "Oh yeah, Marine boot camp. Holy shit. It's really happening!"

"GET UP! GET UP! OUT OF THE RACKS, RECRUITS! GET ON LINE! GET ON LINE!"

I jumped out of my rack as quickly as I could. Wearing my new brown T-shirt, white underwear and "Jesus slippers" (plastic thongs), I got to the foot of the bed and stood at attention. Moving down the line, each of 57 recruits sounded off with his number. I was #42.

We were given bottles, and told to go to the bathroom, or "head," and fill them with urine. In the mad scramble, one recruit dropped his bottle. A DI exploded.

"RECRUIT! ARE YOU CRAZY! OR ARE YOU STUPID? THAT'S GREAT – THAT'S JUST FRIGGIN' GREAT. DROP IT RIGHT IN THE PISS AND SHIT!!"

Me and about six other recruits who were going through some kind of urinary constipation quietly chuckled. It was pretty funny. However, next it was *my* turn for a little DI attention. When I finally finished, I gave my DI the bottle with my piss. He looked at it and said, "WHAT KIND OF FRIGGIN' COLOR PISS IS THAT? WHAT HAVE YOU BEEN DRINKING YOUR WHOLE LIFE – BEER AND SODA?"

Physical training is crucial to being a recruit and a Marine. Recruits are tested upon their arrival at bootcamp in the Initial Strength Test — pull-ups, crunches and a 1.5-mile run.

During Forming Week, we were introduced to our Senior Drill Instructor. Senior Drill Instructors are identified by the black, patented-leather belts they wear. The DIs in their charge wear olive drab belts.

"SIR, NO SIR!" I shouted – but he was exactly right. I had spent my last week as a civilian drinking. The DI was smiling strangely.

"WE'LL FIX YOU, RECRUIT!" he screamed in my ear.

You know, it's funny how, when the DI is yelling, or better yet, directing his fury at someone *else,* it's a laugh riot – but when it's *your* turn, all of a sudden it's a whole different story.

That evening, with 57 guys running out of the bathroom – excuse me, *head* – it was like a riot scene. As we raced for our beds – I mean racks – we must have left a mess in the head.

"Fire watch" is a one-hour shift during the hours of sleep. One recruit watches over the squad bay, the other in the head. Their main duties are to make sure all the recruits are accounted for, as well as their weapons and footlockers. He or she is to report anything unusual immediately to the DI's "house" or office. Who pulls the watch is usually decided alphabetically, or by rack order. Same difference.

Tonight Recruit Perry had fire watch, and during the night he slipped, fell on the floor in the head, and somehow managed to mess up his wrist up pretty bad. For some reason, he woke me up and showed me his injury. Even though I didn't want to get caught talking to him, I could tell he was worried, so I looked at his wrist. It looked bad, and I told him he'd have to tell the DI what happened.

As it turned out, Recruit Perry had suffered a broken wrist. That was *it* for him. No training with a broken wrist, so they sent him home after only *one night* on Parris Island. He must have died of embarrassment when he got home with nothing to show for his training except a shaved head and a broken wrist. With all the rumors about Parris Island, you'd almost want to make up something a bit more heroic than slipping in the head, but oh well. Everything happens for a reason, so I hope it all works out for Recruit Perry.

That night, our platoon was ordered to hit the rack at 1900 (7:00 PM). It was still light out. Good Lord. I have never been so tired in my life. It's weird going to bed when it's still daylight out – especially without a case of beer invested in you. That's what the "old me" was used to – but I could feel the old me slipping away with every passing minute. My head hit the pillow, and in seconds I was asleep.

THURSDAY, MARCH 16

"REVEILLE!"

At 0300 (3:00 am) sharp – the lights went on and we jumped out of bed. "I'll never get used to this," was all I remember thinking to myself. This morning we received our rifles, the M16A2s, and then marched to chow. Marching seems simple when you're watching someone else do it, but it's not so easy to learn yourself. My marching skills need a lot of work. So does just about everything else about me, especially my discipline.

To make matters worse, Parris Island is filled with sand fleas. They are little murderous bugs that suck the blood out of you like a mosquito. They seem to come out suddenly and disappear just as quickly, but when they are around, we recruits have an additional reason to hate life. This morning, after chow, the sand fleas were out in full force, biting away at us. We have to just stand there and *take it* as they bite us – we're not allowed to swat them!

"DID YOU GUYS GET TO EAT?" our DI asked us. "IF *YOU* GET TO EAT, THEN THE *SAND FLEAS* GET TO EAT ALSO." Inside, I laughed at his demented reasoning. In a sick way, it only seemed fair. However, that thought soon passed as another sand flea bit me, and I found myself cursing the little bastards again.

Each platoon has anywhere from three to five Drill Instructors, or DIs, assigned to it. After finishing lunch, we were introduced to our Senior Drill Instructor – Staff Sergeant Bixby. He was very severe, but at the same time he also came off as really cool as he laid down the law to us.

We all sat on the floor, Indian style, as rigid as stone, as he spoke to us. We were intent on making a good impression, not to mention the fact that we were all petrified. We could hardly believe it when he told us to relax. After the fifth request, he screamed, "RELAX, DON'T MAKE ME TELL YOU AGAIN!!"

He continued, "YOU CAME TO PARRIS ISLAND TO BECOME MEAN, GREEN KILLING MACHINES! TWISTED STEEL, WITH SEX APPEAL! SO YOU'LL MAKE ALL THE GIRLS WET WHEN YOU GET HOME! OOH-RAH!" We all let out a little chuckle and relaxed our perfectly straight backs for the first time.

"WELL," Bixby went on, "IT IS MY JOB TO SEE THAT YOU

GET THERE!!"

Aye, Aye to that! Maybe this won't be so bad after all. SDI Bixby told us that our two other DIs would be as tough as nails, but that we should realize that what they're going to do to us is *necessary*, and that it's being done for a reason. Hmmm. Sounds kind of ominous.

Next, we were shipped to the Dental Center to be processed by Navy Dentists. They seemed to enjoy messing around with my teeth. After that, we had the IST, or Initial Strength Test. It was pretty intense. All six platoons in our company, Charlie Company, were present. There were about 20 DIs there. I used to think football practice was bad, with all the yelling and screaming, but nothing really prepares you for Marine Corps Recruit PT (Physical Training). In fact, that's where I first heard the distinct sound of the raspy, machine-like DI voice that's in all the movies and videos.

I didn't dare to even *try* and look the DI's in the eyes. Some things are not worth the penalties, especially with the whole company out there. We did pull-ups, sit-ups and had a mile and a half run. To pass the IST, you've got to do at least three pull-ups, 35 sit-ups and run 1.5 miles in 13 minutes and 30 seconds. I did 7 pull-ups, 47 sit-ups and ran the mile and a half in 12:30, passing all three tests.

You're probably thinking, "big deal," but being in the shape I had allowed myself to get into before bootcamp, I was happy. After the shock of the last few days, it was great to know that I can do something right. For the first time, I felt that if I tried harder than ever before, I just might *make it* here. Lord knows I have the right people to push me.

Six out of our platoon's 56 recruits failed the Initial Strength Test. Tomorrow, these six will have one more chance. Not too much time to prepare. If they fail again, they'll have to spend at least three *extra* weeks training on Parris Island, in what's called PCP (Physical Conditioning Platoon). Another recruit told me that PCP is all exercise, with DIs everywhere screaming at you – supposedly ten times worse than regular Boot Camp. No thanks!

FRIDAY, MARCH 17 (St. Patrick's Day)

Today was our biggest event yet. Our forming DI marched us off to

Recruit Price was never the strongest of runners, and bootcamp made me strive to perform better and faster every time we laced up our "Go-Fasters," a.k.a. sneakers.

our new barracks, our "new home." We were very excited as we marched sloppily about a quarter mile to the barracks. We all bumbled and stumbled as we carried our sea bags, ALICE (All-purpose Lightweight Individual Carrying Equipment) packs, rifles and who knows what else. Thirty minutes later, after we systematically packed away all our gear, we were positioned six across by 10 deep, sitting Indian style once again. Only this time, we *weren't* told to relax.

Our Series Commander Capt. Galant stepped to the front. He read an oath of responsibility, and our DIs swore to obey this oath. He wished us all good luck, then turned the show over to the SDI and dismissed himself. The SDI introduced our other two DIs, Sgt. Parks and Staff Sgt. Wight. One is in charge of teaching us how to march, while the other is responsible for teaching Marine Corps knowledge. Also, there is the "heavy." He's the DI who makes you want to crap your pants the most. Every platoon has one, and I think I can tell who ours is. He got on my case right away. I feel like I can't do anything right.

Our Forming Drill Instructor, Staff Sergeant Ciprioni, taught us the basic skills of marching, skuzz brushing, making a head call, and stuff like that, "the basics of basic," but I'm finding they place a big emphasis on drill here, and I don't seem to be doing very well at it. When you make a mistake – even the smallest kind – they lace into you but good and make you feel ashamed, like a little kid. I made several mistakes drilling, and got reamed like *crazy* for each and every one of them.

And let's not forget our little friends, the sand fleas. Those "suckers" are a menace – they're worse than our DIs. It's hard enough for me to march, let alone stand totally still, without those damn fleas drilling into me. As I gazed out of the corner of my eye to the marshes that surround Parris Island, my mind began to wander. I'm sure I am not the first one to ever consider swimming to freedom – but recalling our DI's warning us of the tide's 17-foot drift, and alligator and shark-infested waters quickly brought me back to reality.

Oh, yeah. Remember the six recruits who failed the Initial Strength Test? Well, they were allowed to take it again today, and three passed. Good for them – or, as our DIs are constantly saying – "Good to go!" As for the other three, it sucks to be them, but we all came to Parris Island to get stronger. After PCP, these guys should all look like Johnny Rambo!

SATURDAY, MARCH 18

Today I got yelled at at least five more times. It's like being in an exploding mine field when the DIs go to work on you, and it's really starting to get to me. They have ways of breaking you down I never even imagined. This morning my bunkmate, Recruit Reilly from Binghamton, New York, jumped off the rack above me and went to get his Jesus slippers. I waited for him – he took forever – then grabbed my sandals and got on line.

Well, by the time I got there, I was "late," and it looked to our DIs like I was taking my time. They exploded on me. I'll never forget the feeling of two DIs screaming simultaneously in each of my ears, like my head was the meat in a DI butt-chewing sandwich.

"WHAT'S WRONG WITH YOU RECRUIT? ARE YOU LAZY?"

"SIR, NO SIR!"

"I KNOW YOU'RE FAT – AND I THINK YOU'RE LAZY TOO! AREN'T YOU?"

"SIR, NO SIR!" I screamed for all I was worth. They make you feel like you're two years old. Like I said, it's really beginning to get to me. They scream at me more than my mother ever did and all I can do is answer, "Sir, yes sir!" What gives here?

We haven't been allowed to take a shower since we got here, and we've also all been wearing the same pair of shit-stained underwear since we arrived. They've got us so terrified of doing anything without being ordered, we thought we weren't allowed to change them. When our SDI found out (he probably smelled us), he laughed and said we were out of our minds. He tells us we could have changed them the first second we got to our barracks.

Instead, we've spent five days in the same nasty friggin' pair. Disgusting. They were so friggin' gross, you don't even want to know. It was totally humiliating. Anyway we were totally relieved, pissed off, yet happier than ever to be throwing on some clean BVDs or "skivvies/drawers." So at least we finally got to change – but still no shower.

The stained glass windows in the Parris Island chapel were all designed and created by Richard M. Gibney, a Marine veteran of WWII who took part in five D-Day landings, including Tarawa and Saipan.

SUNDAY, MARCH 19

It's Sunday, known here on the Island as "God Day." For the first time since we arrived, we were allowed some free time. It was only four hours, but after the non-stop frantic activity of the last few days it seemed like a week's vacation. I used the time to write some letters to Mom, Kirk and Lisa. Then I went to church. For the record, I was raised Roman Catholic, but have never been too religious.

I was surprised at how much I enjoyed church. It was the best service I've ever attended. Instead of the typical Marine exclamation of OOH-RAH, we were shouting OOH-PRAY! We were swaying in the aisles, hugging each other, and singing, "We Got The Whole World In Our Hands," substituting 1st Battalion, 2nd Battalion, etc. for "whole world." It was great!

Also, at the end of the service, we sang the Marines' Hymn. I've never been so moved by a song before. I really don't know why singing the Hymn made me feel so incredible – I guess it's because despite all the screaming, or maybe because of it, I'm starting to feel like I'm part of something for the first time. It almost made me cry.

Oh yeah – the DIs have been calling me fat since I got here, and even though I've been trying to hold in my stomach in hopes they'd stop cracking on me, the scales don't lie. I am officially 6-foot tall and weigh 209 lbs. This classifies me as an official "fat body." They put me on a weight control regimen that includes a special diet, plus extra Physical Training. Great.

Also, all my shirts will have two white horizontal bars stenciled on the front and back of them – "racing stripes." This will mark me as a "fat body." The white bars are intended to let the DIs know who's out of shape and may need some extra attention during PT sessions, but it seems like it's really supposed to shame me into losing weight. At least that's how I feel, so it's already working.

Almost every other recruit here is in perfect shape, and I'm ashamed that I'm not. As for the diet part, it really sucks because I don't get to choose my own food like the rest of the recruits – I have to eat exactly what they tell me to eat. Oh well, if it helps me lose weight, it'll be worth it.

MONDAY, MARCH 20

On the way to breakfast, we marched past a bunch of injured recruits with broken hands, broken legs, and twisted ankles, limping toward the chow hall. It was still dark out, and it was a scary sight to see. They looked like a modern day "Spirit of '76" painting. I wondered, will I end up like this? If it could happen to them, then why not to me? Are a certain percentage of recruits guaranteed this fate, by probability alone?

If you get injured – or if you fail some part of training – you're dropped from your original platoon. All of a sudden, your old "family" is gone and you're what they call a "pick up" when you join your next platoon. Going through this experience, a possibility for any recruit, is a huge reality check. I pray it doesn't happen to me.

I wondered about my eventual fate as I completed the last day of "Forming" for male recruits. Still no shower. I don't get why they won't let us clean up – I've never felt so filthy. Tomorrow is TD-1, our first Training Day.

The DIs are ready to have at us. I get the impression that the DIs aren't allowed to mess with us until tomorrow. I'm getting better at drill, but I know I still need a lot of work – in more ways than one.

Tomorrow, I believe the shit really hits the fan. I'm going to try hard to change my ways, but just before lights out, I told Recruit Pechette I had a feeling that I'd soon be the King of IPT, an extracurricular form of strength training – and a way for the DI's to "get their point across."

This "Racing Stripes" undershirt means that I checked into bootcamp a little overweight. I'm also sporting standard military-issue, unsexy eyeglasses, a.k.a. "B.C.G.s" or "Birth Control Goggles."

PHASE ONE

TUESDAY, MARCH 21: TD-1

"Three minutes to lights!"

"TWO MINUTES TO LIGHTS!"

"ONE MINUTE TO LIGHTS!"

As I woke up at the first screams, my eyes began to focus. All I could see were silhouettes of three men, standing perfectly erect, except they're not standing still. Their bodies were gliding through the barracks as if they were ice-skating. I knew it was my DIs from their "Smokey the Bear" covers (hats). Seeing them move in this truly inexplicable manner gave me the chills. It's crazy, but it gave the impression that the DIs were supernatural.

I could sense the tension as recruits stared nervously at the blackened DI figures, just as the DIs awaited anxiously. Then, at 0500 (5:00 am) sharp we heard a loud, thundering, "LIGHTS, LIGHTS, LIGHTS!" sounded by the Fire Watch Recruit, and the lights went on. Training Day One was finally upon us.

"GET UP! GET UP! GET YOUR STINKIN' BODIES OUT OF BED, RECRUITS! LINE UP!"

I jumped out of bed in my underwear – oops, I mean I jumped out of my rack in my skivvies. I've got to remember to use Marine terms at all times – they go ballistic if you don't! I was moving slowly, and Senior Drill Instructor Bixby started screaming at me right away.

"GET DRESSED RECRUIT! NOW! NOW! HURRY IT UP!"

I was still groggy from getting up at 0500, and Bixby's booming voice scared the living daylights out of me. I knew they yelled at everyone in the Marines, but I hadn't been prepared for so much fury to be focused directly on me. I felt like I was doing everything wrong, and my every mistake was being noticed immediately, as if a microscope was on me. Nervously, I put on my cammies and boots as fast as I knew how, then stood at attention at the end of my rack, waiting for my turn, as each recruit sounded off. My platoon is made up of guys from all over the East coast, mostly Pennsylvania, Florida and New York – 36 White, 8 Black, 7 Hispanic, and 1 Vietnamese.

"RECRUIT NUMBER 41, PRESENT SIR!" (I was now #41 instead of #42, due to the absence of the four recruits we lost.)

After we were all present and/or accounted for, the platoon made its first official head call. We still weren't allowed to shower, and they didn't even let us alone in the head. It was a large open room lined with toilet stalls that had no doors, and in the back were the shower stalls with no dividers. There was no privacy whatsoever. Everything is right out in the open.

"HURRY IT UP!" I could hear Bixby screaming. So, after the fastest crap I ever took in my life – I didn't even have time to glance at myself in the mirror – I raced back out to get on line thinking, "God, I'll never get used to this." We stood there, terrorized, waiting for more orders. By now we were deathly afraid to do anything without being ordered to. Stupidly, I moved out of attention position to glance at DI Parks scream at another recruit. I noticed a few others doing the same thing. We didn't get away with it. Parks's radar must have been working overtime.

"ALL RIGHT," he wailed, "WHO'S LOOKING AT ME?"

My heart was pounding like a runaway locomotive as I sounded off.

"SIR, THIS RECRUIT WAS LOOKING AT YOU SIR!"

I waited for the others to say something, but no one else spoke up. I was the only one that admitted it! DI Parks raced over to me.

"FOLLOW ME BOY, GET YOUR NASTY ASS DOWN TO MY PIT!

"YES SIR," I screamed.

Even though it was my first trip to the "pit," I knew instinctively where to go. The "pit" is a large sandbox found right outside each squad bay at Parris Island, as well as other random spots. Ours wasn't huge, but that day it was big enough to me.

"PUSH-UPS NOW!" He ordered.

"PUSH-UPS, AYE SIR!" was my conditioned response. I dropped

down and started pumping away. The first 50 or so weren't too bad – but everything after that was pure torture.

He saw I could barely do another pushup. "LEG LIFTS, NOW!" he roared. I immediately switched to leg lifts, forgetting one little detail: I hadn't repeated the order. Well, as you can imagine, my pit session went on for quite a while. It really was a "joyous" experience that everyone should go through. Well, at least I can say I was the first recruit in my platoon to get the shit thrashed out of him. I have a funny feeling, it won't be the last time it happens to me.

"ALL RIGHT," Parks told me as I finished, "BACK INSIDE! YOU'RE LUCKY I'M FEELING GENEROUS, PRICE – THAT WASN'T NEARLY ENOUGH!"

I know I was only down in the pit for around 15 minutes, but I tell you, if anyone can make 15 minutes seem like 15 months, it's a DI. As I stood there, locked at attention, making sure not to look at Parks, I suddenly got the feeling that he and I were going to be spending a lot of "quality time" together.

We marched off to breakfast. Afterward, we had some classes in Marine Corps history and traditions. In the afternoon, we did Table PT. Man, was *that* an experience. All three platoons were lined up surrounding a table that's approximately 7 feet by 7 feet, and stands about three feet off the deck (floor). Then the Series Gunnery Sergeant or Series "Guns" jumps up on the table and in a huge BOOMING voice he greets us, "GOOD MORNING FIRST BATTALION!"

We returned his enthusiasm, "GOOD MORNING, SIR!!"

"OH, HELL NO! I THINK I SAID, '**GOOD MORNING FIRST BATTALION**!!'"

Man we screamed our asses off in response. After a while he was satisfied, and ready to begin.

"YOUR FIRST EXERCISE OF THE MARINE CORPS DAILY SEVEN WILL BE SIDE STRADDLE HOPS (jumping jacks), SIDE STRADDLE HOPS IS A FOUR-COUNT EXERCISE. WE WILL DO 15 OF THEM."

"IS THAT ALL SIR?" We were trained to ask.

"HELL NO, WE WILL DO 25 OF THEM!!

Crunches and sit-ups play a major role in becoming "twisted of steel." Here, Recruit Price is finishing a maximum set of sit-ups in a two-minute period.

"IS THAT ALL SIR?" Our reply, once again.

"YES, THAT IS ALL, BUT DON'T LET ME CATCH YOU WHISPER-
ING TO ME LIKE I WAS YOUR SUZIE-Q BACK ON THE BLOCK.
SOUND FRIGGIN' OFF!!"

"YYEESS SSIIRR!" We screamed so hard there was spit was
flying everywhere.

"I WILL COUNT THE CADENCE, YOU WILL COUNT THE
REPETITION, STARTING POSITIONS MOVE (we spread our feet, hands
on our hips), READY... ALTOGETHER EXERCISE... 1... 2... 3... "ONE"...
1...2... 3... "TWO" (etc.)"

The next exercise was Marine Corps push-ups. In between exercises,
they had us run in place and scream at the top of our lungs. It was wild.
"GET YOUR KNEES UP, GET EM UP," yelled a DI right in my face.
"SOUND OFF, YOU DISGUSTING LITTLE TURDS!!" was shouted at
some recruits in the back row. This went on as long as it took for the
Series Guns to be satisfied that he was getting max participation. This
was the program for every exercise.

Next were flutter kicks, leg raises, mountain climbers, and a couple of
others I can't remember. I do remember the leg raises killed me. "SIX
INCHES," yelled the Series Guns, as we were made to hold our legs
straight out and hovering six inches above the deck. If they even saw *one*
recruit with his feet on the deck, they would not let us recover, a.k.a.
stand up.

Then we did the Circuit Course and ran two miles. After all the PT
beforehand, that run was hard as hell. I was out of breath the whole time
– it really kicked my ass, but I didn't want to let the other guys see me
quit, so somehow I managed to finish the whole run without falling out.

"This place is going to kill me," I thought.

At 1930, came the long-awaited shower. We all lined up in front of our
racks (beds) as usual, and DI Parks yelled, "TAKE OFF YOUR
UNIFORMS!" Everything here is a competition – even showering. They
divide us in nautical halves, starboard side, the right, and port side, the
left. Whoever undresses first gets to shower first. The rest have to shine
their boots and belt buckles. My side stripped down to our underwear

first, so we got to hit the showers first.

"STARBOARD SIDE, SHOWER UP," the DI yelled, "PORT SIDE, SHINE 'EM UP!" The platoon then echoed the order and carried it out.

While the other side started to shine their shoes, my side raced to the shower. It was another mad dash as 25 sweaty, stinking recruits raced to the showers. Trying to ignore the embarrassment of being totally naked with my fat stomach hanging out, I lined up to hit the showers. I somehow managed to get under a shower nozzle first, and was shocked to discover it was spraying only cold water. I had always hated cold showers, but they had gotten us so filthy and made us wait so long for this shower that I didn't care. I guess they planned it that way. First they change your behavior, then they change your attitude, then they train you to accept – and even welcome – the changes they've made in you. You don't have any choice in the matter.

As the recruit next in line immediately started shouting, "Hurry up" at me, I started scrubbing like a madman. After about two minutes, I jumped out from under the nozzle and lined up at the mirror. When my turn came, I slopped some shaving cream on my face and started shaving. Looking at myself in the mirror was like looking at someone else. I didn't recognize my own face. I was as bald as a newborn baby, and felt completely exposed.

It was like no shower routine I had ever done. There was no hair to comb. There was no deciding whether to shave or not – we have to shave every day. There was no need to worry about making my sideburns even – they were also gone, along with the rest of my hair. I almost nicked myself about ten times shaving, then quickly brushed my teeth. The whole operation took a total of only five minutes. I've never showered and shaved so fast in my whole life, I thought as I raced back out to shine my boots. This was the routine we'd be following every night from now on. They even inspect us every night before we hit the rack, to make sure we're properly clean.

Afterward, we got an hour of free time that raced by like a New York minute. I wrote letters to my mother, father and Kirk. Then it was time for hygiene inspection. Everybody lines up in their skivvies, holding their arms out, bent at the elbow, with their palms facing up. The DIs go down the line looking us over. When they come to you, you have to spin yourself all the way around like a little gear in some huge machine – so they can inspect every inch of your body – and you sound off on your condition. Even if I really had a minor medical problem, I wouldn't want to say so. I wouldn't want to look like a wimp in front of the whole platoon.

"RECRUIT PRICE HAS NO MEDICAL OR PHYSICAL PROBLEMS TO REPORT AT THIS TIME SIR!" During the first two weeks, I would come to fear saying even this short little sentence in front of our "heavy." The heavy is a slang term for the DI who takes on the role of enforcer. I mean, one little screw-up and he's on you like stink on shit. To him, the tiniest error is a personal insult.

After every recruit was inspected, we were given a brief moment for prayer. Then, we were ordered to mount our racks – at the position of attention. It's as if we were standing at attention and just fell over into our racks, frozen like statues.

"GOD, COUNTRY...CORPS!" SDI Bixby shouted.

"GOD, COUNTRY... CORPS!" We all repeated, screaming at the top of our lungs naturally. This followed by the command and our repeat reply, "READY, MOUNT."

We had to stay in attention position in our racks until we were given permission to get under the covers. Bixby waited a few minutes and then gave the command.

"AAAAAADJUST!"

"ADJUST, AYE SIR!" We boomed back.

The lights went out. It was 2100. I started to think, I can't believe I'm doing this, but I was so dead tired I fell asleep before I could finish the thought. Once again, the Marines had planned well. We were being trained to keep ourselves "Marine clean" at all times, and they made sure we were too tired to do anything but accept it.

WEDNESDAY, MARCH 22: TD-2

"Three minutes to lights!"

"TWO MINUTES TO LIGHTS!!"

"ONE MINUTE TO LIGHTS!"

"LIGHTS!"

"GET UP! GET UP! OUT OF BED, RECRUITS! LINE UP!"

They got us up same bat-time, same bat-channel – 0500. When I jumped out of my rack, I told myself I wasn't going to get DI Parks mad at me again. There was just no way I could take his screaming in my face again. And things did go pretty well all day, until we went to combat training. I "screwed the pooch" big time, when asking to make a head call.

"Sir, may I have permission to make a head call, Sir?"

"I? I? 'I' IS NO LONGER! RECRUIT, GET DOWN AND START PUSHING! I'M TIRED OF TELLING YOU TO REFER TO YOURSELF ONLY AS 'THIS RECRUIT!' DO YOU THINK YOU'RE SPECIAL OR SOMETHING?"

"NO SIR!" I shouted while doing push-ups. I was already on about 45 of them.

"YEAH? WELL, I'M GONNA GET YOU LATER. I'VE GOT SOMETHING FOR YOU!" he screamed. I dreaded to think just what that "something" would be. I mean for crying out loud, I had drunken so many canteens of water – I had to pee so bad I couldn't even think straight. I somehow managed to do 50 push-ups without dying. It still hurt, but it seemed a little bit easier for some reason. From there, we went back to the squad bay to set up for Physical Training. PT is hard for me, because my body isn't used to such strenuous exercise – although if I keep messing up and having to do push-ups, I'm sure it will get used to it in a hurry.

I'm convinced Drill Instructor Parks has it in for me. I keep messing up his drilling, and he takes special pride in his close order drills. It's going to take time and 110% concentration to master drill. "Drill is a thinking man's game," DI Parks keeps reminding us. I could be in trouble.

I'm trying very hard to do what's expected of me, but it's incredibly difficult. I've never had so much expected – *demanded* – of me. On today's 2-mile run, Recruit Grant collapsed. And he's the son of a Marine Sergeant Major! At first I thought he was faking, but he actually did suffer some kind of attack. They took him away and did God only knows what with him. Several other recruits are also slightly hurt. I had no idea so many would drop out so quickly. It's a rough world here – I'm just trying to survive. To think I had once boasted it would be easy!

This afternoon, we were marched to the barbershop for another haircut. I couldn't believe it was time already – my hair had barely begun to grow back after last week's shaving. Platoon 1082 lined up outside the barbershop, and DI Parks started barking orders at us.

"PUT YOUR STINKIN' COVER IN YOUR CARGO POCKET! BUTTON YOUR TOP BUTTON, AND TURN YOUR COLLAR INWARD! NO TALKING! FIRST RECRUIT, INSIDE!"

The first recruit on line ran inside and plopped down into the chair, which was facing away from the mirror. We aren't permitted to watch as our heads are shaved, unlike in the movies. Thirty seconds later, that recruit was as bald as the first night we arrived on the island. My turn came soon after, and once again that buzzing razor was all over my head, or "grape" as the Marines call it – and, in seconds, I was totally bald again. Those barbers are definitely NOT paid to be gentle.

I can't believe we have to get haircuts every Wednesday. I can understand why they don't want us to have long hair, but to have our heads viciously buzzed to the skin by a clipper every single week seems like overdoing it. And they even charge us for each haircut – a total of $72 dollars will be deducted from our pay for all the cuts we'll be getting. I think we'll only be allowed to keep some hair on the tops of our heads near the very end of training – they call that a "high and tight." This cut is a very big deal, because it shows that you've made it to the end of the ordeal, and are about to graduate and become a Marine. Seems VERY far off.

I was covered with stink and sweat from exercising, running and marching all day, not to mention getting a million hairs down my neck from the haircut. I could not wait to jump in the shower. Once again, I didn't care how cold it was. I just accepted it. After another record-fast shave, we had hygiene inspection and assumed the position of attention in our beds.

Tonight there was no order to "adjust," and we were too afraid to get caught moving. So we all fell asleep at attention. They're even making us *sleep* with discipline!

THURSDAY, MARCH 23: TD-3

Recruit Grant came back to 1082 today. He couldn't tell us what happened to him after he fell out yesterday, because he had no memory past collapsing and waking up with the medics at the hospital. Our Senior told us the standard procedure: First, they dose you with freezing ice-water, to reduce your body's temperature, then your clothing is removed and you're put in a tub of ice water. Then they stick a thermometer up your ass! They call it a silver bullet. Turns out Grant was okay, so he was allowed to stay with the platoon and come back to drill with us.

I did pretty well during drill, and DI Parks didn't really yell at me too much. That's not to say he didn't yell at me at all, though. He told me again he's going to "get me." Uh, not good at all.

We went to a PT session after drill – they really motivate you to improve. PT was the hardest yet. They worked our recruit asses off. At the end of the Circuit Course is a two-mile run. The CC, as it's referred to, consists of a combination of push-ups, sit-ups, lunges, crunches, curls, etc. If you drop out three times, you're screwed. Today, one of our recruits, six total out of Charlie Company, dropped out. Not much sympathy was given to them by the DIs.

Tomorrow is our first time boxing each other. It's the only boxing training we'll get before our first competition against the other platoons. That comes in two days. The platoon that wins the boxing event gets a trophy and a red flag. Hope our platoon kicks some ass!

FRIDAY, MARCH 24: TD-4

We marched to chow 15 minutes early today. From there we marched to "Leatherneck Square," Parris Island's version of Mad Max's Thunder Dome. We learned four different ways to kill a man, including choke-holds, arm locks, and violent boot-stomps to the head. MOTIVATE!! Of course, this type of killing is for combat and defensive purposes, only. Next, came boxing. MORE MOTIVATION!! Around here, if you don't like to fight, it's almost unpatriotic – like not voting. No guts, no glory!

I boxed Recruit Palarino. We slugged it out pretty good. I took a few

The DIs at bootcamp were hard on everyone, but they always set such a great example, both physically and mentally, that we constantly aspired to become like them.

shots in the head, but gave a bunch more back. Recruit Grant made out much worse – his Parris Island story has just about ended. Today he had a noticeable lack of motivation, proving he just doesn't have what it takes. He was ordered to report to the SDI, and he practically ignored him. I thought the Senior was going to blow a gasket. Recruit Grant and his trash(all his belongings) were gone before lunch. Later for him. SDI says he'll get bounced around from platoon to platoon for a while before he actually leaves.

"UNCLE SAM NEVER LOSES! DON'T MESS WITH HIM!" SDI Bixby roared at Grant.

Bixby only yelled at me once today. Maybe I'm finally starting to get with the program. I hope so – I'm giving it everything I've got. I've never put so much effort into anything in my life.

SATURDAY, MARCH 25: TD-5

Today, DI Wight took charge of us. He gave us a pre-test on Marine Corps history. I thought it was pretty easy. Some of the other recruits did horribly, though. I think they're clowning around too much. They don't have the right attitude, and I feel this is going to become a big problem soon. If they (we) don't shape up, Wight is really going to let them (us) have it, and I hope he does. Listen to me, complaining about other people's lack of discipline.

We called today "Mike Tyson" Day, because Mike gets out of jail today, and we're scheduled to have boxing matches against Platoons 1080 and 1081. I got in there and fought like hell! I won the first round, but lost the next and last in a close decision. My nose got busted up pretty good. There was blood all over my shirt, but luckily no real damage – that is if you don't count my ego.

Man, you should have seen Recruit Chidester fight! He's a real bruiser. Even though his man outweighed him by 25 pounds and the gloves are padded, he hit his opponent so hard he knocked him right the hell out. The SDI was so happy he gave Chidester a 15-minute phone call home! Tell me there isn't a guy in the world who wouldn't want to call home and tell their pops or brother, "Yeah, I hit this guy so hard, his whole family probably felt it!"

Despite Chidester's performance, unfortunately, we lost as a platoon. But we'll get them next time. Actually we were robbed, but you don't need to hear me bitch and moan about it.

After boxing, we trained with our M16A2 with M7 bayonet. Bayonet training was crazy. They had us chanting, "KILL, KILL, KILL!" to keep us really aggressive. I have to admit, it felt awesome to be so focused, with all the guys screaming. I really got into it.

We spent the rest of the day in class learning about snakebites, insects, and Marine history. The instructor asked us questions during a slide show. He told one recruit from another platoon to stand up. In front of him was a huge, huge wall with a slide of the Marine Corps motto, Semper Fidelis, projected on it. The instructor asked the recruit to tell him what the Marine Corps' motto was. He didn't know! The classroom, full of about 300 recruits, was in complete horror. This mental midget stood there for about three minutes, dumb-founded, until the DIs let him have it. Thank God it wasn't me. I'll bet it was a long day for that recruit.

SUNDAY, MARCH 26

"God Day" number two. DI Wight had us again this morning. We ate chow and then came back to the Barracks. Four hours of free time (OOH-RAH!!) is like a lifetime now. During free time I wrote five letters, to Mom, Kirk, Jenifer, my Uncle Bob and Aunt Wendy, and my Grandma Kay – then I folded my laundry. It was the first chance I've had to think in a week – the pace of bootcamp life is incredibly hectic.

I realize that even for all the screaming DIs and hell they give us, I'm actually starting to like it here. I enjoy the camaraderie of my fellow recruits – they're all interesting people, and they all have a story to tell. Some are a little too cocky for their own good, but who isn't from time to time? This morning, Recruit Clayton, a really stubborn guy from Cleveland, Ohio, asked permission to make a head call.

"CAN IT WAIT A MINUTE?" the DI answered as he walked away.

"AYE SIR," Clayton said.

But then Clayton went anyway, when no one was looking. He just blatantly disregarded the DI. Guys like him are going to bring the DIs down on the whole platoon. I have a feeling there is a runaway train loaded with respect and discipline headed right at Platoon 1082. Look out!

MONDAY, MARCH 27: TD-6

Recruit Clayton *did* get in deep shit, and that's cool with me. I never thought that I'd be glad to see others punished for breaking the rules – but that's what they're instilling in us here. As I predicted, the heat is being turned up. Drill Instructor Parks was lecturing us about something today, and a few recruits – including me – failed to pay enough attention (a.k.a. "gaffing him off"). Unfortunately he noticed, and he went on the warpath.

"IF YOU PEOPLE ARE NOT GOING TO RESPOND TO THE EASY WAY," he screamed, "THEN I'M GOING TO SHOW YOU THE HARD WAY! NOW – WHO WASN'T LISTENING TO ME?"

Two recruits stepped out of line – I was the third. I knew it was going to mean punishment for me, but I had to do it anyway. I'm learning how to take responsibility for myself here, and it was just something I had to do. It was a matter of integrity. I couldn't lie. That's just not who I am – at least not anymore.

And I was right – Parks quickly punished all three of us. Man, did he work us out hard. He PTed us so hard it got downright painful, but when I was done it felt good to know that I had owned up to my mistake, been punished for it – and now it was over. It felt real good. Parks seemed to ease up on me afterward. Thank God. I couldn't have taken much more punishment.

My marching is coming along slowly but surely. Some of my fellow recruits are just not getting it. They are more pitiful than me. They don't seem to even be trying. Parks is about to really lose it on them – they may even be dropped. We got the results back from our knowledge pre-test. I found out I aced it – I did the best out of everyone. As a reward, I got made leader of a study group. Some recruits did so bad on the test, I don't know if they'll even be able to finish boot camp. One got only 10 questions right out of 40, while another got only three out of 40. What the f--- oops, I've been told that recruits aren't supposed to curse – I mean, what the heck? Anyway, if they can't pass the test eventually, they'll be gone for sure.

We spent this morning in the swimming pool. You've got to jump in wearing your cammies, with all your gear and carrying your rifle (actually a plastic rifle that weighs the same as a real one). There are different levels of swim qualification. I made CW-3, but since I'm going for a job in the infantry, tomorrow I'll be required to try to improve to CW-2.

In the afternoon, we had inspection by SDI Bixby. We got all decked out in our cammies and had to stand at parade rest position (at ease) forever. The platoon wasn't dismissed until each recruit passed inspection, which started at recruit number one. About 50 minutes into the inspection, Recruit Burton dropped to his knees and collapsed right on his back. Apparently, if you lock-up your legs for a long time, your blood circulation gets cut off and then – WHAM – you pass out.

I'm recruit #41, so I had to stand totally still for about 70 minutes. It sucked. I thought I was going to pass out myself – but I held on, managed to not lock up my legs, and didn't move the whole time. And to think I used to never be able to sit still for even five minutes! I guess I'm finally learning some discipline. "How about *that* trash?"

TUESDAY, MARCH 28: TD-7

Today, we jumped out of our racks and busted right into Physical Training. First we kicked a little Table PT. Then it was on to the mighty obstacle or "O"course. The "O"course is about 200 feet long and is a series of – you guessed it – obstacles. On one, there are bars about seven feet up that you have to climb over, as well as walls and logs to run across, but the kicker is the rope climb at the very end. It is about 20 to 25 feet up. Once you reach the top, you sound off your name and platoon number, and then your DI will tell you to climb your ass back down. Surprisingly, it all went very well, until the rope. Yeah, I admit it. It kicked my butt. I just couldn't get to the top. I was winded and just ran out of gas. From there, we did an individual 2-mile run. At least the runs are getting easier for me.

In the afternoon, we went back to the pool. Since my Military Occupational Specialty or MOS was infantry, I was required to try for CW-2. I entered the water and passed the first part of the test, a 50-meter swim in full combative gear. I was really proud of myself. I felt like one of an elite group, because not too many people could do it, about a 15 percent passing rate. The second part, however, was a different story.

We were supposed to do the sidestroke 25 meters while dragging another recruit, then drop him off and swim back 25 meters on our own. I tried three times and got further each time, but I just could not get it. I have to pass it in order to graduate infantry, my preferred MOS (Military Occupational Specialty).

It was a physically draining day, but a good one all in all. I'm upset about not passing. Not getting CWS-2 was the only mark on an otherwise superb day. I'm not going to let it get me down, though. I'll get it sooner or later.

A recruit hurt his shoulder pretty badly today on the "O" course, so he'll probably be dropped soon to MRP (Medical Reconditioning Platoon). Recruit Lange got into another fight – there's something really wrong with his thinking. And Recruit Donner may have to go to PCP. He looked truly pathetic trying to get even three feet up the rope. It was ugly.

I'm sorry to see anyone fail. There's a real camaraderie developing among our platoon. I don't want to see anyone leave, especially if they're going to PCP. We hear it's a real hell,
but the reality of it is, it doesn't matter *what* we think. If it has to be done – it is. Period.

We picked up a new recruit today. His name is Stillwell. He failed the First Phase knowledge test, not once, but twice, so he got transferred to our platoon and in the process dropped back from TD-17 to TD-6. He's cool with it, though. I know I'd be pissed. He seems to be pretty locked-on. I think his experience is going to help Platoon 1082.

I stepped on the scale tonight during our hour of free time. I've lost eight pounds, and gone from 209 to 201. At this rate, I'll lose 48 pounds by the end of boot camp. Good to go! I know a lot of it is water weight, but it still feels damn good

WEDNESDAY, MARCH 29: TD-8

"Another glorious day in the life of the Marine Corps," Recruit Martin told me, as we were about to step off after finishing morning chow. I had

With the right amount of exercise, proper diet and constant "pounding of water,"
it was not long before Recruit Price started to shed some weight.

to agree. The rising sun was giving the sky an awesome purple-orange glow. After chow, it did feel a little nippy, though. Maybe that's because we were on our way to Physical Training in our little green shorts. When I say those shorts are little, they're about one step up from panties.

Don't sweat it though, you get used to them. First, we did Table PT and then, the Fartlek course for the first time – the Fartlek, so unpleasantly named, is a combination of about two miles of running, while stopping every quarter of a mile to do all kinds of torturous cardio-vascular exercises. Surprisingly, I didn't do too badly. Senior Drill Instructor Bixby made it fun by having us repeat some really amusing cadences.

After PT, we did rifle maneuvers in the squad bay for about an hour and a half. Going over the basics. "PORT ...ARMS," "RIGHT SHOULDER... ARMS," "LEFT SHOULDER...ARMS." The day was going pretty well and then came, "INSPECTION ...ARMS!" This is a seven-count movement that we just can not seem to get in sync for. The movement is used to show the inspector that your weapon is clear. To return to a closed bolt weapon, the command "PORT...ARMS" is given again and what is supposed to happen is everyone slides the bolt home and closes the port ejection cover altogether.

To help us learn, the DIs gave us ditties to keep in tune with each other and we were just screwing the whole deal up. Over and over and over, and we'd still have two or three guys clicking in late. We were getting frustrated, but our DIs were about to have heart attacks. After about 45 minutes, a recruit on the port side of the formation must have been daydreaming, because the ditties for the seven-count movement were simply 1...2...3...4...5...6...7... So where this recruit came out with the number 8, I'll never know!?!

"WHO SAID THAT?" DI Parks roared.

No one answered.

"WHO FRIGGIN' SAID IT?"

"ONE MORE TIME, WHO FRIGGIN' SAID GOD DAMN 'EIGHT'??" Our heavy looked like he was about to explode. "NO

ONE. GOOD TO GO, GOOD TO GO! LOCK YOUR WEAPONS TO YOUR RACKS, TAKE YOUR BLOUSES OFF AND GET YOUR NO-INTEGRITY, SLIMY ASSES TO MY PIT!!"

We knew we were in for it now. All the recruit, whoever he was, had to do was own up. I couldn't wait to find him myself. To make a long story short, we were thrashed to no end and still no one came forward. One recruit finally owned up to it, but the heavy knew it wasn't really him. "GET INSIDE, GET ON LINE, AND STAND FREAKIN' BY!!"

After a long wait, Recruit Banks, the real culprit, stepped forward. He admitted to his mistake, WAY too late though. Banks was forced to watch while our SDI, Bixby, punished the rest of us for Banks' mistake. They do that to make you feel really guilty, and to get the whole platoon on your case. Just like the movie "Full Metal Jacket," and the whole jelly doughnut thing.

"THANK RECRUIT BANKS," SDI roared.

"THANK YOU RECRUIT BANKS!" we answered.

"WHAT DOESN'T RECRUIT BANKS HAVE?" SDI asked.

"INTEGRITY, SIR!" we screamed.

"I CAN'T HEAR YOU!"

"INTEGRITY, SIR!" Again and again, we thanked Recruit Banks for his lack of integrity.

Then the Senior proceeded to thrash the hell out of us. Some of the guys thought it was stupid, but I thought it was a good lesson. A good Marine needs integrity more than his M16. You know what I mean? If you don't, then boot camp is definitely not for you. If it had been me, I would have felt like the biggest dirt bag on the island.

Later, I went back to the pool again, to try to qualify CW-2. I failed again – I actually did worse than the first time. For the better part of the afternoon, myself and about 20 other contract infantry - men, who were being forced to upgrade, spent our time in swim lessons. It was a very discouraging experience, but now I'm more determined than ever to pass.

After that, since it's Wednesday, we marched over to the barbershop for yet another haircut. I'm starting to understand the purpose of our recruit haircuts. They take away a part of our old lives and attitudes, and give us one less thing to think about. With everything else we've got on our minds, I'm actually glad I don't have to think about my hair anymore. Five minutes every night to shower, shave and brush my teeth doesn't leave much time for such shit – er, I mean, such trash.

When it was my turn for a cut, I jokingly told the barber, "Good afternoon, Sir!" He just looked at me funny and proceeded to buzz me bald for the third time. Oh well, at least I'm getting used to it. Our cold PT showers and hygiene inspections are becoming routine, too. They've even got me so that I don't feel right unless I shave every night. Good old Mom will never believe the changes going on in her son.

THURSDAY, MARCH 30: TD-9

Today really was a glorious day – and it had nothing to do with sunsets. Today's PT activity was Pugil Sticks at Leatherneck Square. Pugil Sticks are long poles with heavy padding at each end. that are supposed to simulate an M16A2 service rifle with an M7 bayonet affixed. We put on protective gear – football helmets and stuff – then get in a pit two at a time and thrash it out with each other, jousting with the sticks. It can get very intense. Today though, Platoon 1082 really kicked ass.

There's nothing like looking into another man's eyes and sensing his fear. I fed off it, like a shark, as I lunged at my opponent with everything I had. I was all over him with "death blows" and I quickly won all three rounds. We went in scared, but most of us came out feeling awesome. It felt great to turn around and see your Senior's proud face and get congratulations from the other recruits, as well. BAM, POW, POW – like an episode of Batman!

When it was over, we had won the red flag, which is given to the platoon that wins the competition. We marched back to the squad bay with the flag flying in front of us. It gave me, and all of us, a feeling of intense pride. Platoon 1082 was beaming.

From there, I went to the pool again. This pool was becoming a freakin' aqua-nightmare on Elm Street. I didn't want to go – but I knew I

Recruits battle each other with Pugil Sticks to simulate close combat with rifles and fixed bayonets. Platoons who win as a team take home a trophy, bragging rights, and a much happier SDI..

had to conquer this test, which has given me so much trouble. My first try I failed again, and almost gave up on myself. I was very down, and I totally lost my "military bearing," as they call it. I was pissed – but the instructors weren't about to let me quit. The Marines push you and push you, and you either get there or you're out. So, I got some more lessons and was told to try again, in the afternoon.

I had a lot of time to think it over during chow. I was looking at four more days of this crap. I mean I know it's good for me, but I was turning into a prune, and being in wet cammies all day sucks. Plus I hated being separated from the rest of the platoon. I made up my mind. Today, it ends. This time, I was determined to make it.

I paddled my life away. I swam 50 meters with rifle, helmet and flak jacket, and then towed another recruit 25 meters, paddled back 25 meters and back another 25 meters with two rifle packs – all in full uniform and gear. Recruit Lish and I were partners in swimming. Guess what? I FINALLY PASSED! So did Lish. We felt as if we had won our own personal war.

The whole experience was incredibly rewarding. I mean for the last three days, I didn't think there was any way possible I could make it. Then all of a sudden, here I am, I did it. I really did it. I was so happy with myself I couldn't help but smile – I never even thought to see who was watching, so when I looked up and saw the look on SDI Bixby's face, I froze. He was instantly on my case.

"PRICE! WIPE THAT FRIGGIN' SMILE OFF YOUR FACE OR I'LL DO IT FOR YOU!"

With that little warning, I managed to stop smiling. But I will always remember the important lesson I learned today: No matter what happens – NEVER GIVE UP! I was smiling all day, however, I kept it on the inside. Gotta run – after shower, shave, and shine, I've got to press my cammies and look sharp, or SDI Bixby will have my ass.

FRIDAY, MARCH 31: TD-10

Today was comparatively slow. We prepared for testing and initial drill. We also lost three more recruits by the time we hit chow: Recruit Jordan (drugs), Recruit Reed (shoulder injury and drugs) and Recruit

Stanley (nightmares and drugs) are all gone – just like that. Apparently, they must have taken drugs in between their medical screening and getting on the bus. Hope it was worth it for them. Either way, Platoon 1082 is now down to 51 recruits. The sad thing is, they've already been forgotten. On Parris Island, you don't have any time to worry about the past, because there's so much going on minute-to-minute that will determine your future. It's human nature to care about your fallen comrades, but if you spend too much time worrying about them, the next thing you know you'll be *one of* them. Somewhat like being in combat, I imagine.

We got some more shots from those Navy squids today – one in the shoulder and one in the butt. Hollee! After the tookie shot, the docs made us all sit in line with our "BUTTS-TO-NUTS." A phrase I *am* allowed to say, and an order I carried out only by being very secure in my manhood! We were then told to rock back and forth for about ten minutes. The swaying back and forth would help rub the pain of the shot out. Apparently, this one was a doozie.

Watching us doing this must have been pretty hilarious. Our whole platoon was walking around with sore butts the rest of the day. I could only imagine how we would have felt if we hadn't done that ridiculous rocking deal. The biggest bonus of getting shots (for the fellas) was getting up close to the female Corpsmen or Navy "Docs."

Other than that, though, I really feel great. It's only been two weeks, but I already feel much stronger. I can also feel my attitude changing. This shit is definitely working on me. Tomorrow – a mock PFT test, to see where we stand.

SATURDAY, APRIL 1: TD-11 *(April Fool's Day)*

I'm kind of upset because we didn't get to play an April Fool's Day Joke on Senior Drill Instructor Bixby. I suggested that the whole platoon get up before wake up call and hide in the shower. Then when he came to get us up, we'd all be "missing." It was a stupid idea anyway – we would have paid dearly had we done it.

The mock PFT went really well for me this morning. I've improved my pull-ups from 7 to 10, my sit-ups from 47 to 69, and went from a 1 1/2 mile run at 12:02 to a 3-mile run at 22:50. Not too shabby, eh?

Tonight, we got to watch television for the first time in almost three weeks. We finally got another cable to the TV after the old one got stolen, (we guessed by a DI from another platoon.). Appropriately enough, a news clip of Marines in Okinawa, Japan, was on TV. We were all talking and joking, but everyone quieted up real fast when that clip came on. It's as if we've already bonded to those Marines.

Afterward, SDI Bixby gave us a long talk before we mounted our racks. He's starting to make himself accessible to us on a human level. This allows him, and us, to open up to each other. His philosophy is to break us in gradually. If we f--- up – I mean *screw* up – then we pay for it. If not, then things continue to go smoothly.

SUNDAY, APRIL 2

We're encouraged to go to church on God day. However, today, DI Parks told us that we are here for a *reason*. He wants to instill personal initiative in us, so we don't just do our jobs, but excel at them. "YOU RECRUITS HAVE TO LEARN TO **SACRIFICE!**" he tells us. I suppose training 158 out of 168 hours in a week doesn't count? Anyway, he's right.

With Senior Drill Instructor's inspection and Physical Training getting more intense, we do have a lot to get prepared for. I never realized how much I could appreciate just a few hours of down time. Now, four free hours every Sunday seems like a whole weekend. I sure as hell hope life isn't this hectic after boot camp.

The rest of the day was spent studying for the First Phase Knowledge Test, and drilling, drilling and more drilling. I knew that DI stood for Drill Instructor, so why I was surprised to be doing so much drilling, I don't know. Some guys freakin' love it. As far as I'm concerned, they can have it.

MONDAY, APRIL 3: TD-12

Today was one of the busiest, toughest days yet. We started off learning more LINE, a method of hand-to-hand combat. From there, we moved to Pugil Sticks II on the bridge. If you lose, it's a simulated 500-foot drop to your demise. I was pretty nervous as I put all my protective gear on. You really don't want to screw up with everyone watching and all. As nerve racking as it is, once that whistle blows, its show time – just you and another recruit, mano-a-mano. Instantly, adrenaline replaces the fear.

As I approached my opponent from the other platoon, I admit I was scared. Yet, when we locked eyes, I saw he was more scared than I was! In that instant, I knew I was going to win. My confidence soared and I began delivering blow after blow. We battled it out, and I won my match.

You should've seen Recruit Chidester! Again, he was simply awesome. He was like lightning with a stick. The recruit he was fighting came at him high and hard. Chidester very calmly ducked his blow, and watched as his opponent gathered his balance right at the edge of the platform. I don't think anyone will forget the viciousness of the blow that Chidester landed right under this poor sap's chin. It seemed like that other recruit was almost airborne for a second, before he landed on his back.

The Senior promoted Chidester from a squad leader to our guide – leader of the platoon. Our old guide is pissed, but everyone knows Chidester deserves it more. The old guide was only guide because he could drill all right, and no one else really stood out until now. Oh yeah, I almost forgot, you guessed it – Chidester got another phone call home! I think this time, he called his Susie-Q (a.k.a. his girlfriend). Lucky dawg! Butler still, we won as a team. The red series flag stays with 1082. It felt awesome to be in the winning platoon, but that feeling was soon forgotten in another busy day of drill and PT.

We messed up drill in the afternoon. We just need to concentrate and relax. SDI Bixby was so pissed he sent us to the "pit" for punishment in the form of intense physical exercise. Then we drilled some more, and went to PT. We did three sets of max sit-ups and then two sets of max pull-ups. I was up from seven to ten in only two weeks.

Then we did what is called individual group runs. The platoons break down into sub-divisions based on running performance. If you run a 19-minute, 3-mile run, you join the 18 to 20-minute group. Since I seemed to be on a roll, instead of joining my standard run-time group for the 3-mile run, I said, "Hey, let's go for it" and volunteered to move up to a quicker group. At the time I did it, I felt proud, but soon I felt stupid. It was damn tough trying to keep up with the faster recruits – I thought I'd never make it. I really sweated it out, but when it was all said and done, though,

Recruit Price made it. OOH- RAH! Not only are the DIs pushing us, but I'm pushing myself. What's going *on* here?

TUESDAY, APRIL 4: TD-13

This morning we took medical classes. I now know how to correctly use the "Heimlich" maneuver, make a splint, a tourniquet, make a stretcher out of a poncho and two sticks, and give a solid dressing. After the test, we began marching to practice for Initial Drill. For the first time, I'm happy with my marching.

"A LO DODDY LEFT, A LO DODDY LEFT, A LEFT FOOT RIGHT, A LEFT FOOT RIGHT," SDI Bixby was singing like a bird, and that was music to our ears.

Soon it was time for our next lesson, LINE II, a form of Aikido and jujitsu that's extremely deadly when used correctly. "Grab, twist, grab, switch, twist, grab, kick, place, sweep, smash," or something like that. The smash is a heel right down on the mask or skull eye area. This is done while pinching back the attacker's elbow and arm, which you've already broken. Awesome, is it not? All you need is violence, intensity and discipline, followed up with a whole lot of practice.

These Marine instructors are very effective at their jobs. They are a 110% asset to the Corps. There's a few Combat Instructors that look like they could defeat small armies by themselves. The Marines definitely are the best friggin' warriors on earth, and I'm starting to feel very proud that – *if* I work hard enough and don't screw up – I will someday be one of them.

WEDNESDAY, APRIL 5: TD-14

As soon as we woke up – BAM! We ate chow, cleaned house and got right to PT. Today was our PFT (Physical Fitness Test). I had a dream last night that I did 18 pull-ups. Back in reality, I could only manage 11. That's still one better than I did last time, so at least I'm heading in the right direction. My sit-ups are up to 75. Five more and I'm an 80 man. Eighty sit-ups equals a perfect score of 100 points, 20 pull-ups is another 100 points and an 18-minute 3-mile run is another 100 points for a total perfect score of 300 points. My run time dropped down again, this time to 21:55. My total score was about middle of the pack, around 250. As a platoon, we scored best and won the PFT as a platoon, thus keeping the Series flag in our hooch. We are the best!

Later, we practiced more drill, and in the afternoon, while 1082 did the Confidence Course, I got sent to dental. The dentists are really cool, especially the one who worked on me – Navy Commander Coils. While in the chair, I heard music on a radio for the first time in almost four weeks. Pink Floyd and the Steve Miller Band never sounded so good. The best part was just being able to relax and talk to someone. I never dreamed I'd think of going to the dentist as relaxing. Boy, the things I used to take for granted.

I did feel kind of sad, because being at the dentist, I missed doing the Confidence Course. But fortunately, I was not as down in the dumps as Recruit Cacciola from Massachusetts, who was sent to us from MRP. He's a good guy – a contract infantryman, like me. We had joked around about drinking our first brew at Okinawa, Japan, together.

During the "Slide for Life," a slide down a 45-degree, taut rope strung over a pool of water (maximum height 25 feet), Cacciola fell about 15 feet and re-dislocated his shoulder. Unfortunately, that's an automatic bus ticket home, and at least a nine-month wait to try again. He really took it well though. Probably better than I would have. He promises to come back in nine months, after he heals. His courage, not to mention his commitment to the Corps, motivated the hell out of me.

After my "vacation" trip to the Dentist, I rejoined 1082, and we marched over to the barbershop for our weekly haircut. I already don't mind getting a recruit cut anymore – I've been here on Parris Island for almost a month now, and I've almost forgotten what I used to look like with hair. At first I didn't understand why the haircut was necessary, but now I can't see it any other way. There is no reason we need all that nasty hair getting in our way all the time. What is happening to me here? Is recruit Price learning to think like a Marine?

Well, we've got a big test, plus Initial Drill, tomorrow. If we fail the test, we can't become Marines. However, if we fail the Initial Drill, I don't think we'll even see tomorrow. DI Parks takes drill *very* seriously.

THURSDAY, APRIL 6: TD-15

Today was a huge day – Initial Drill Test. Everyone was humming with fear, excitement, apprehension – you name it. On top of everything, it was pouring rain. This is only the second day we've had rain. I hope it's not an omen or something. No problem – we're ready for anything, so we got decked out in cammies, covered by ponchos.

I thought the written IKT (Initial Knowledge Test) was pretty easy. There were a couple of tricky questions – and a couple that we weren't even taught thrown in there – but I still kicked it. Recruit Price got a 93%. Platoon 1082 had the best average in our company, and got a big trophy for it. Two of our recruits failed the written test. The two other platoons each had several more failures.

Then came the big worry – Initial Drill itself. I was really nervous. With the rain continuing, we conducted Initial Drill inside. Some platoons went before us and did terribly. Some recruits even dropped their rifles, the ultimate sin. There is nothing like the sound of a rifle hitting the deck, especially when you're inside a gym, in complete silence. We cringed at the sound, as if it were nails scraping a chalkboard, yet at the same time we were happy, because we knew it helped *our* chances of winning the event.

When I got out there, I was shaking like a leaf. Uncontrollably. My palms were extremely sweaty and the look the Series Guns gave me as I snapped a rifle salute and could not stop my hand from quivering. What a wuss, huh? But we ended up doing all right – Platoon 1082 lost Initial Drill by only one friggin' point, 61.7 to 60.7. The other platoons weren't even close. I think DI Parks was given the rest of the day off by the SDI, just so he could cool down. He really put his heart and soul into preparing us, and between feeling cheated by the graders, and let down by us, he was pretty irate.

FRIDAY, APRIL 7: TD-16

It's about 1000, and Platoon 1082 is packing up its gear. We're just completing the first phase of Recruit training. Our ALICE packs (backpacks) are full, and tomorrow morning we head to a new barracks nearer the rifle range. They say it's about a five-mile hike, and we'll live there for about two to three weeks. Everyone is pretty loose, with the pressures of Initial Drill and the First Phase testing over. Yet, as we pack all our worldly possessions into a couple of bags, in a funny way I feel like we're preparing to go to war. Maybe we are. They say the rifle range can be extremely difficult to master. But I've heard that if you just pay attention and follow directions perfectly, you can qualify as an expert, no problemo.

We met PMI (Primary Marksmanship Instructor) Corporal Stevens, the evening before we were to leave for the rifle range. He seemed really cool. I'm worried about qualifying since I've hardly even handled a weapon, but I know I just have to be confident. Without confidence, it'll be just like when I thought I couldn't qualify in swimming.

Out of the gate, Platoon 1082 gave PMI Stevens the proper and thunderous respect he was due as a United States Marine. To our surprise, the first thing he told us was, "Don't sound off! After hearing rifles going off all day, I just want to relax, go out, and have some 'brew-skows'." (I love all the awesome terms and lingo Marines use. They're classic.) PMI Stevens gave us a few pieces of advice, and said he'd be seeing us.

SATURDAY, APRIL 8: TD-17

As usual, the lights went on at 0500, and Senior Drill Instructor Bixby was right in my face.

"GET UP PRICE!" he yelled, "GET UP!"

Today is the big hump (march) or as the higher-ups call it, an "administrative move" to the Weapons Barracks. We were "late" getting to morning chow because the other platoons cheated by waking up early. Believe it or not, this is against regulations, so SDI Bixby was pretty pissed off. Because of it, we were the last to fall out for the move. After chow, we packed up our gear and started the five-mile journey around 0700.

During a hump, there are many things you have to consider. It's not like walking to school with all your text books. You've got a lot of gear, about 45 pounds worth, plus your trusty rifle, "Betsy" (if you choose to name her that), and you also have to ensure that you're as comfortable as possible – from the fit of your helmet strap to how your back straps feel on your shoulders, right down to your socks and shoelaces. These simple comforts are important when you're in a "forced march," because a forced march is one where falling back is not an option.

Something that's only slightly discomforting at first can dig at you steadily, resulting in serious injury after 10 miles. Also, you have to keep about 40 inches between the back of the guy in front of you and your chest, or else you might hear, "REACH OUT AND TOUCH SOMEONE, MAGGOT!" Let me tell you, you don't want to be the sluggo who drops back to where you can't reach your bud's pack in front. If you are, I hear the Navy is looking for guys like you.

In all of our formations, height dictates placement. Taller recruits are in front, down to the short, short men in the rear. Having longer strides makes marching easier. Being 6-feet tall, or 72 inches in Marine metrics, I was one of the taller guys in the platoon. But, I still had problems keeping my 40 inches of space. Those "short, short" guys in the back of the formations must have had a real fun time humping while cussing under their breaths at us recruits up front.

Just before the halfway point, Recruit Knox and I got sent to the back of the formation for failing to sound off our knowledge loud enough. Being all out of breath and physically drained is not really the best time to scream out all the knowledge you've learned, to help strengthen your "brain housing group." And wouldn't you know it, as luck would have it, I end up right next to DI Parks.

Right away, he started ripping me a new butt. He got me pretty nervous, telling me how he was going to "get me," over and over. The whole rest of the way I was hoping he'd bother someone else. No such luck – I am starting to face up to him though. He doesn't scare me as much as he did when I was new here on Parris Island. Sure he doesn't!

Once we got about a quarter mile away, we double-timed it to Weapons Barracks. It was an all out speed hump now. The whole rest of the way, Platoon 1082 was a mess. We weren't sounding off properly, and when we did finally arrive at our "new home," we were moving too slow to suit the Senior Drill Instructor. To punish us, he ordered us to make our racks, but gave us so little time to accomplish the task, we would have had to have set a new Guiness World record.

"I am nothing without my rifle..." Perfecting rifle movements such as right shoulder arms, port arms, and inspection arms takes endless practice, repetition and teamwork.

We didn't get it done on time, so we had to rip the beds up and do it again, and again, and again. Then came our footlockers. Bixby had us dump all our stuff in our footlockers out on the floor, just like in the movie "Full Metal Jacket," and then made us re-pack them.

Everyone's stuff was all mixed together. Cans of Brasso, (a brass polisher), and shoe polish rolling everywhere. The only way it could have gotten worse is if a friggin' jelly donut fell out of my foot-locker. We just grabbed everything as quickly as we could, and sorted it out later. A few recruits weren't squared-away, dirty clothes and crap, so they got pulled to the quarterdeck for some "motivating incentive training."

The quarterdeck is an area outside the DI's living quarters in the squad bay. Every time a recruit is told to go there it means they have "displeased" a DI in some way, and will probably have to do PT until they're ready to bust a gut. It's a bit barbaric, but it's damn effective.

After Bixby finished yelling at us – for the moment – he marched us to the rifle range. We went down range to the butts, the area behind the targets, to learn the scoring system. Then we went back to the 300-yard line to learn different firing positions. There, PMI Stevens was waiting for us.

He gave us instruction about the rifle range and the fundamentals of marksmanship, then we practiced, hands-on. He made us do everything about a hundred times – he says learning to fire a rifle is all about repetition. He says, "It's a craft, a skill and a religion." Whatever it is, I'm going to give it everything I've got. Anything less and I'd only be hurting myself. When it starts getting boring, and everyone is tired and wants to go chow down – that's when I know I need to dig deep and give it more than ever.

SUNDAY, APRIL 9

It's almost 0800 on Palm Sunday. Some recruits are shuffling off to church, some are writing letters; some are spit-shining their boots. Others are doing push-ups, and practicing snapping-in with their

M16A2 rifles. The four hours of free time we get on "God Day" is so relaxing it's like a dream. I can't emphasize this enough.

Today went pretty smoothly, as do most Sundays. After free time, we climbed the ropes and for the first time, I finally made it to the top. OOH-RAH! I finally realized what I was doing wrong. I was using way too much arm strength. Turns out, it's all in the legs. You just use your legs to grab the rope, then inch on up.

Unfortunately, seven or eight recruits couldn't make it. Bixby was pretty pissed off. He promised them they're "in for it" as they floundered around on the ropes, looking like sacks of you know what. They were pathetic. But I guess I shouldn't be so hard on them – a while back, er, I mean a few minutes back, that was *me.*

Today, I volunteered to be First Squad leader for the week. It's a program the DIs use to make sure everyone gets a chance at leadership, at least once. I think this will help me gain more self-confidence, and I am going to try to lead by example.

Thinking back, I'm horrified at how much time I wasted before coming here, just drifting through life without making any effort. F--- that! There's no way I'm going to let history repeat itself. Instead of saying, "I should do this" or "Maybe it would be a good idea to do this," I am going to simply DO, DO, DO! No more half-stepping through life for Recruit Price. This is the start of a new life for me.

So ends Phase One!

During "Grass Week" recruits will have to sling their rifles, load up all their gear and hump six miles to a new barracks by the rifle ranges. (This photo was taken during a 10-mile hump at Camp Geiger's School of Infantry in Jacksonville, North Carolina.)

PHASE TWO

MONDAY, APRIL 10: TD-18 "GRASS WEEK"

OOH-RAH! Recruit Price has made it alive (and let's not forget kicking) – to Phase Two! Today is our first official day of Phase II, starting with Grass Week. We did another seven-mile hump, then more "snapping-in," or settling into firing positions, with our M16A2 service rifles, and "dry firing" them. Snapping-in and dry firing are virtually the same thing. You learn trigger manipulation, proper breathing techniques and how to acquire a good sight picture, all of this without a single round being fired.

Practicing all the different shooting positions can be very boring and uncomfortable. We also learned all about sight-zeroing and aiming. I'm working on my form, and trying to qualify as a marksman – an expert marksman, preferably. They say that patience, stamina and motivation are the keys.

During our march back to practice after chow, I accidentally dropped my rifle, the ultimate sin. My friggin' sling-keeper slipped right off and – BOOM – it hit the deck. I thought DI Parks was going to have a heart attack. He keeps telling me he's "going to get me." It hasn't happened yet, but after dropping "Betsy," I may have just earned a death sentence. Sometimes I think he just wants me to worry about it. Well, he's said it so many times that even though it does continue to rattle me, I'm brushing it off quicker now. Hope my theory is right.

After we finished rifle training, we PTed. We ran two miles in our cammie bottoms and leather boots with our rifles. Today felt like one of the warmest days yet, and I think many other recruits agreed. As we ran, recruits were constantly falling out of the run – some collapsed to their knees, some on their backs. It was hard seeing them like that, but it did give this recruit motivation to keep going. So I did, and I made it. Five recruits from 1082 were not so lucky. Even though we won the

PFT Strength Trophy, we still had the most run drops. Recruit Donner, who collapsed, may be heading out of here to the dreaded Physical Conditioning Platoon. We keep hearing that PCP is like a living hell with DIs on your back every minute of the day, and nothing but PT. This is a nasty fate, and I feel bad for Donner because he's a good kid – but he just doesn't have the stamina to cut it with the rest of us. They say, "Whatever doesn't kill you, only makes you stronger," so maybe PCP is the best place for him.

TUESDAY, APRIL 11: TD-19

Training Day 19 out of 57. We are one-third of the way home! This morning during PT, the sweat was pouring off of me, dripping all in my eyes, but it felt great. After calisthenics, we ran the three-mile course. My time was 21:55 – exactly the same as last time. This is good news, because it means that the last time wasn't just a fluke. Next time, I know I'll do even better.

We received our usual weekly haircuts one day early this week because we'll be on the rifle range tomorrow. Man, those barbers are not gentle – they really jerk your head around while they're clipping you. I used to get all tense having my head shaved – but this was my fourth recruit cut, and by now I've learned to relax and keep my neck real loose while he buzzes me. Getting a haircut every week doesn't bother me at all anymore.

During free time, I went to work out some more, then set out my cammies – I'm on fire watch tonight. Fire watch is one hour of guard duty that rotates between recruits every three nights, based on the size of the platoon. You pull different shifts every time – tonight, they'll wake me up to relieve another recruit at about 0200. It sucks to lose a much-needed hour of sleep, but somebody's got to do it. Tomorrow is a big day – we shoot the M-16 for the first time!

WEDNESDAY, APRIL 12: TD-20

Well, it finally happened. Today, we fired our M16A2 semi-automatic assault rifles. Talk about power – it was friggin' awesome! We fired three magazines of five rounds each. I was in the first row of recruits to

The "World Famous Starlight Range," where Platoon 1082 learned how to fire the M16A2 Service Rifle. Recruits learn every aspect of the skill, including breathing, trigger control, and weapon safety.

fire. We locked on to our targets, which were 36 yards away. My target was one of three little bull's-eye pictures or "dog" targets. No worries, it's not actually a picture of a dog.

When you fire at the target, the basic idea is to try and group your shots together as tightly as possible. You get your sights aligned, then your sight picture, then BAM – using your best trigger control, you fire! Well, my first rounds were a total waste. I was so enthralled with actually firing the M-16, I forgot all the correct procedures – my breathing, everything was wrong. What really distracted me was the smell of the carbon. My previous experience with guns was nil, but after breathing in the smell of carbon from firing a rifle for the first time, I was in love!

I fired off all my rounds, and my shots hit everywhere but the target. PMI Stevens had to test-fire my weapon to check it out. Of course, I thought, it *had* to be the weapon. How bad could I be? But when PMI Stevens tested my rifle, his grouping was practically the size of a quarter. Apparently, Recruit Price is no "Dirty Harry."

Stevens was pretty pissed because almost 25 percent of us were off on our groups. It made him look bad, as though he had been a bad teacher, but I think the truth is that we were just bad listeners. Some guys got confused and even fired on the wrong target. At least I wasn't *that* confused. The PMIs had some left-over rounds, so they gave them to me to fire. My last four rounds were pretty good – this recruit had three shots in the black (bull's eye), but one shot was out of my grouping range. Tomorrow, I'll get another chance.

THURSDAY, APRIL 13: TD-21

Holee! The days are flying. It feels like I just arrived at Parris Island just a second ago. Today was our second straight day on the "World Famous Starlight Range." We did almost the same exact thing as yesterday, but today I got better grouping with my shots. I almost forgot, that the basic idea of firing from only 36 yards away is to BZO your weapon or "Battle-sight Zero" it. This is just personally customizing your weapon, by making elevation and wind adjustments on it. If any of this sounds confusing, don't sweat it. If you ever find yourself on a Marine Corps rifle range, all you have to concern yourself with is doing exactly what the PMIs tell you. They teach it much better than I could ever regurgitate it. Anyone who absorbs the principles of their teaching will become an expert, no problem.

Tonight, like every night, we had Mail Call. Mail call here – like everything else – is strictly regimented. Every night all the recruits sit on the deck (floor) and wait for their name to be called.

"PRICE!"

"HERE SIR!" I yell at the top of my lungs.

Then, you get up and haul ass to get your letter. You've got to hold out your hands in front of you, parallel to each other, with about a half-foot of space in-between. When the DI takes your mail and puts it in-between your hands, you've got to slap it as hard as you can, and scream, "MAIL RECEIVED SIR!" If you don't pound it hard enough, they abuse you some more by keeping the letter and make you wait until later to get it.

Getting food in the mail? Not a good idea. Mom and Dad, this is no summer camp! When recruits receive food in the mail, if they are lucky, it's just taken from them. If they are not so lucky, they have to eat it *all*, right on the spot. This evening at mail call, Recruit Fowler received food. Guess what – he got four huge bags of Reese's peanut butter eggs, and they made him eat it all. Talk about indigestion. We all thought it was a riot, but Fowler didn't seem to share our opinion.

Anyway, today I received a disposable camera in the mail from Kirk. He's dying to see some pictures of me as a recruit, but that trash is not allowed. DI Bixby took the camera away from me. He was cool though – he told me he'd give it back to me at graduation.

FRIDAY, APRIL 14: TD-22

Oh man, did this week fly by. Unbelievable. We snapped in about 400 hundred times. Some positions require a tight grip with the sling wrapped around your bicep. If you're serious about hitting the target, the sling will leave some hickey-like marks and bruises.

As far as strength training, today went great. I did 15 pull-ups and

78 sit-ups. The Marine Corps' (and my) goal is 20 and 80, to get the maximum points for promotions. I'm on the way. After some intense PT, I finally completed the entire "O" course for the first time. I did it! Ten recruits were not so lucky – including Recruit Donner, who is (yes) still with us. He looked awful out there.

The poor guy looked like he was going to die right there on the rope. He did keep trying, but the truth of the matter is if you don't get up that rope the first time, it only gets harder. So in the end, it was all Donner could do to just hang there with his big old gut hanging out. I think Bixby is pulling for him, but he looked really nasty today, and proved he's still got a long road ahead of him. Yet at the same time, it seems like Donner is a cat with nine lives.

We also took a test on Rifle Knowledge today – I got a 90, but several people failed. SDI Bixby says they're "in for it." We also learned some new marching movements today, cleaned our rifles to get them ready for inspection tomorrow, and PTed with Bixby.

Ever since we had a recruit pass out while at the position of attention, I'm constantly worried about locking up my legs and hitting the deck. Well, today I kept them *too* loose.

"PRICE!" Bixby screamed at me, "STRAIGHTEN UP THOSE LEGS!"

"Aye sir!"

"WHAT? LOUDER! YOU RECRUITS AREN'T SOUNDING OFF LOUD ENOUGH!"

"AYE SIR!" I wailed.

Bixby really knows how to make us work – I don't think I ever yelled, "AYE SIR," so loud in my entire life! And after that, I tried like hell to remember not to keep my legs too loose. Gotta run – tomorrow morning we have another seven-mile hump.

SATURDAY, APRIL 15: TD-23

During today's hump, I marched behind Recruit Shales, just like when we are in drill formation. He's another good kid, but it's common for the DIs to torture him, because he messes up a lot. He's constantly getting pitted – they make him sit against the wall and hold his M16A2 straight out at arm length forever. At least he's getting stronger, but he pisses DI Wight off – thus Wight hasn't let Shales speak to him in three days.

Anyway, today I was about three inches from Shales' head at one point in the march. I watched as a huge sand flea parked right on his neck. It filled up on his blood like a car at the gas station. I could actually see the little bugger get bigger, and then fly off satisfied. I wanted to smack it off for him, but with DIs around, you're not allowed to swat 'em – you've just got to bite the bullet and let 'em chow down.

And how did I do on the march? Don't worry sport fans, I made it. A seven and a half-mile hump can't break Recruit Price. We stomped all over the place. However, we suffered the same fate as yesterday because a few lame-asses don't want to sound off properly. SDI Bixby was singing cadences, and people just weren't getting loud. This was most likely due to fatigue, but in the eyes of the SDI, it was a sign of disrespect.

"SOME OF YOU NASTY RECRUITS CAME HERE," Bixby raged, "JUST TO BE ABLE TO HAVE THE HONOR OF SAYING THAT YOU'RE MARINES. BUT UNLESS YOU GIVE 100% YOU'RE GOING TO BE OUT ON YOUR ASS! YOU'D ALL BETTER STRAIGHTEN OUT BY TOMORROW – OR ELSE!"

OOH-RAH for SDI Bixby! He was so right when he said that some people come here just to be able to have the honor of saying that they're Marines, but they don't want to earn it with blood, sweat and tears. Well, no way. They don't give that away for free. You have to earn it.

Because Bixby's intensity is going up, some recruits are starting to get hard on each other. It's like a pecking order. The trash flows downward from the top – the only problem is us recruits are at the bottom. We've been getting on each other's cases about lack of discipline, kind of like policing our own ranks.

A couple of times already, I've lost my bearing and wanted to just unleash on some of my fellow recruits. But, I took a step back, realized that what I was doing was wrong and stopped myself. I never used to have such control over my temper before. Parris Island's "magic" is really working on me.

I knew the Marines would be competitive, but I didn't understand how fanatical it would be. First and mainly, there is yourself. You're constantly pushing yourself to be better and attain self-worth. Next comes your bunkmate.

If he just did 20 pull-ups or did great on a test, and asks you how you did – you want to say you did better. On the flip side, if you just lost a boxing match or something, you keep your mouth shut and hope no one asks how you did. This intense competition is really bringing out the best in me and helping me to push myself to do better.

We also compete with our main foes, Platoons 1080 and 1081. In the First Phase, we kicked their asses. When your platoon does well, your fortune is another platoons' misfortune – this in turn, raises each platoon's dislike for the others. The DIs encourage this competition, like feeding a fire. Lately, things have been tense between platoons – words have been exchanged as we clamber down the barracks stairwells in the morning.

The other day, DI Parks was pissed off at Platoon 1081, or maybe their DIs, for some trash. So when we got to chow hall, he shouted to us, "WHAT DO WE THINK OF PLATOON 1081?"

As he told us to, we spelled out "B-I-T-C-H-E-S!"

"WHAT DOES THAT SPELL?" he asked.

"BITCHES!" we screamed. I couldn't believe we got to do that, but we did. OOH-RAH!

The Donner saga continues. Even after disgracing himself on the obstacle course, he's still with us – in body at least. I think he knows it's just a matter of time until he's out. He was one of five recruits who got punished by DI Wight for leaving their footlockers unsecured – he made them dump all their gear out of their footlockers and put it all in their sea bags – a huge pain in the ass. Their trash is still in there. Meanwhile, I was a little sore from the 7.5-mile hump, so I decided to stretch out against the wall. Wrong move.

"PRICE, WHAT THE HELL DO YOU THINK YOU'RE DOING?! GET YOUR DOG-GONE GRUBBY FEET OFF MY BULKHEAD!!"

I got quarter-decked for that one. Oh well, at least it's better than a pit call. You don't get sand all down your back and everywhere else. And as I was putting my blouse back on at my footlocker, that incredible feeling of accomplishment, adrenaline, and survival felt *so* good.

SUNDAY, APRIL 16 *(Easter)*

We all woke up at 0445, after a pleasant nine-hour sleep. We get an extra hour of sleep on Saturday nights. It's all part of the weekend extravaganza. The 33 of us waited outside the squad bay for the bus, and then went off to church. Easter service wasn't what I expected – there were a lot of officers there, so the chaplains toned downed their usual enthusiasm a lot.

Mass was given outside, on the parade deck, and I thought the best part of it was getting to watch another great sunrise. This time, we were able to relax while it was happening. It would take one bad-ass DI to thrash you during church services. Plus you'd have to be insane to disturb Easter service anyway.

After church, we talked with some guys from Platoon 1080 and found out that they're going through the same tortures as we are – and then some. It was good to hear of their pains, because it helps your morale to know that you're not alone. If the guy to the right and left of me can make it, then so the heck can I.

When Mass was over, we piled on the bus like a bunch of sixth graders on a school trip, and returned home. We were happy to find out that while we were gone, the recruits who stayed behind had a quarterdeck session and a field day, which is a Marine term for a general clean-up of the squad bay. When I was told of all the fun they had without us, I told one of my buddies, "Too bad we missed it, bro, but Happy Easter, just the same!" Reporting his reply is unnecessary. There are already enough dirty words in this diary.

Before our nightly hour of free time, 1082 had a motivational meeting amongst ourselves – the most effective one yet. A lot of good things were said, and the message is FINALLY being hammered home to some of these nasty recruits. We decided that our punishments should be "all for one," meaning that if one of us screws up, we ALL will be punished for

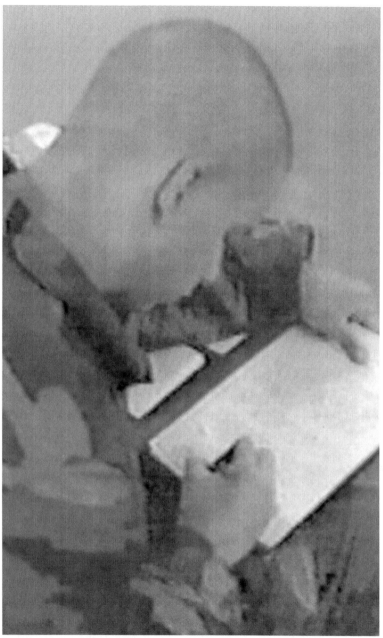

Letters are your lifeline to home when you're in boot camp. I never wrote so many in my life — and I never got so many back in my life, either! There's nothing like the support of your friends and family.

it. Our DIs didn't seem to think that would last long, but they laughed and said, "Have it your way!" We seem to go in cycles – highs and lows. After tonight's meeting, we're definitely on a high. Platoon 1082 is locked on, and everyone is pumped to qualify as an Expert Marksman. I know Recruit Price is.

I'm losing a lot of weight – veins are beginning to pop out, and I can feel myself getting stronger – but it's not enough. Recruit Valdes and I decided to work out like madmen during our hour of free time to build ourselves into super Marine recruits.

Before racking out, I wrote letters to Kirk, and a girl Valdes knows. Hope she writes back – I saw a photo of her, and she's *hot*! No need to worry about Kirk writing back – he's like Old Faithful and a blue-chip stock combined. The Marines have taught me that reliability is a great characteristic in a man. One I intend to work hard on possessing myself.

MONDAY, APRIL 17: TD-24

Today is our first official trip to the KD course – that's Known Distance, or rifle course to you nasty civilians. We were "gently" awakened early, today, and then we had chow. At 0445, it is still nightfall on the Island, so the stars and moon are out in full force. Not only can you see every star in the sky, but the moon is so bright that if you didn't know better, you'd think it was the sun.

At 0600, we were briefed on the butts, or pits – the area where the targets are. Our job was to operate the targets for other recruits who were shooting. Operating consists of raising huge targets up and down, disking the scores, and pasting up the bullet holes for the next shot(s). It was kind of fun actually. We spotted, marked, pasted, raised and disked targets for almost three hours – at our $1.50 per hour salary, that's $4.50. DI Wight pitted me for putting pasties on the carriage, so they would be easier accessed to cover the bullet holes in the target. Even though he punished me, I think he was highly amused. I think he's starting to like me.

We had to eat bag lunches (bag nasties are back) while waiting to shoot – I practically ate my chow through the bag, I ate it so fast. Then I took my turn on the "World Famous Starlight Range." There's a certain advantage to being in the fifth and last relay, because you have a chance to see the mistakes made by the groups before you, and then you can avoid making them yourself. There are 48 targets altogether. Since I was shooting at target number 24, that put me right in the middle of the range – right next to all the coaches and officers. This made me a little nervous, but before I knew it, I was hitting bulls' eyes – and had no complete misses. Good to go!

The hardest part was keeping my data book. This is a data entry book to help you keep an eye on where your shot groups are. Based on your data, you make elevation adjustments and traversing corrections from previous wind conditions. Some of the good old boys just used "Kentucky windage." That's aiming a little to the right or the left of the bull, and letting the wind do all the work. It's basically like guessing, but if you learn the formulas for correction and apply them properly, they say you will qualify as an Expert, no problemo.

Another benefit of shooting on Target 24 and being in the middle is that you are right next to the Control Tower. As luck would have it, I was elected as a Tower Recruit. Myself and four other recruits had to push the tower from the 200 to the 300-yard line, then from the 300 to the 500-yard line.

Even though the tower is on wheels, it was still damn hard pushing that friggin' monster. We had to push as fast and hard as we could, while these redneck corporals were mushing us ahead like we were a pack of dogs! We also had to clean up everyone's garbage bags from chow.

During today's Pre-Qual firing, we were not supposed to keep score at all, because we're supposed to have just concentrate on our marksmanship – but my score today would have been a 200 (er, if I had been keeping score, that is). A 220 is the score needed to be classified as an expert. I'm determined to get expert, but it won't happen with shooting like this.

We got back to the barracks around 1500. As usual, some recruits got in trouble and were quarter-decked. Following the "all for one" punishment policy we agreed on last Sunday, our DIs pitted all of us. They worked us extra friggin' hard on purpose. They wanted to break us from our new policy – and did it pathetically easily. SDI Bixby explained why they had to change our minds. "IF THE RECRUITS WHO KEEP MESSING UP AREN'T SINGLED OUT, THEY DON'T LEARN FROM

THEIR MISTAKES! THEY DON'T GROW!" he said. I realized that while we were coming together as a unit, he was right.

TUESDAY, APRIL 18: TD-25

Back on the range again – same beautiful moon, same stinkin' chow, and same crazy butts. First thing we did was stage and line up the targets. I was right next to the sound booth, with everyone right in front of me. Wouldn't you know it – those damn sand fleas were SWARMING around me like mad, and I forgot to put the "Skin So Soft" lotion (the only thing that stops the damn things) my mom had mailed me on my head this morning.

With no hair to stop them, the sand fleas just dug right in. I was going crazy for about 10 minutes – CRAZY. I hate those damn fleas more than anything. Pushing that friggin' tower again today really sucked too. Looking for spent brass shells in the grass was no picnic either, but it was the closest thing to an Easter Egg hunt I'll see this year. The thought kind of cheered me up in a sick way. Dare I say, "A sick *Marine* way?"

In the afternoon, the DIs asked for "ten smart recruits" as volunteers – my cue. We had to keep score for recruits from 3rd Battalion who supposedly cheated on their rifle qualifying. It felt good to actually be doing work that was official, and not just for practice. We hustled our butts back down to the butts, where the targets are located down range and went to work. We disked and pasted frantically at first, trying to give our shooters good service, which can be critical to shooting well

Unfortunately for the first recruit to fire, it did not matter. The first relay choked – he got a 188, which is 2 points short of passing. The second relay needed to get one more bullseye to qualify. He had a 185 and needed the 5 points a bull would give him. I got so excited rooting for him that even DI Wight noticed.

Wight looked at me and asked, "Are you having fun, Price?"

DI Wight was talking to me like I was almost human. That caught me off guard, and I didn't know what to say. Being the wise-ass that I am, I said "I'VE HAD BETTER TIMES, SIR!"

Wight was not amused. He told me, "WE'LL SEE IF WE CAN'T **MAKE** IT BETTER – DROP AND GIVE ME 30 PUSH-UPS!"

After I finished the 30 push-ups, he yelled "THIRTY MOUNTAIN-CLIMBERS NOW!"

Mountain-climbers are like push-ups. You're on the ground supporting yourself with your hands, but instead of raising your body up, you're running in place while keeping your hands on the ground.

Thirty mountain-climbers later, I looked up and asked, "SIR, DID HE HIT THE BULL'S EYE SIR?"

Wight semi-smiled at my enthusiasm and answered, "Yeah, he got it." I was happy for him – 2nd relay passed. Just then, the 3rd relay recruit's bullet hit the edge of a dirt mound nearby. Dirt and rocks sprayed the targets, and we all jumped a little. It was a quick reminder that being behind the berms is *not* fun and games, but serious business. I almost forgot, 3rd relays' round was no accident, he had countless misses of the entire target. This is actually hard to do. He was awful.

At mail call tonight, Recruit Nix's mom sent him some cookies. Instead of making him chow down on all of them right away, SDI Bixby had mercy on him and us, and let us all eat some. I never knew how much I missed sugar until it was taken away from me on Parris Island.

WEDNESDAY, APRIL 19: TD-26

Day three out on the Rifle Range, and the damn sand fleas are out like clockwork. I swear there's someone on the Island controlling them – they wait until all of us recruits are outside, then press a button that opens a big box full of 'em, and they attack us. A swarm started biting my head. I ignored them for a while, but finally I just couldn't stand it anymore. I broke down and scratched my head.

Now, when you're in a group of a hundred recruits, you would think a tiny movement by one person would go unnoticed. In reality, it is the exact opposite. Since everyone is so rigidly still, a quick flick of the hand is amplified a hundred times over. So, naturally, I didn't get away with it – this time it was Series Gunnery Sergeant Simpson who caught me.

"WHERE ARE YOU FROM RECRUIT?" he ran over and screamed.

The famous statue of "Iron Mike," memorializes the ferocious spirit the Marines displayed at the Battle of Belleau Wood. It was during this battle that the Germans gave Marines the nickname "Teufelhunden," which means "Hounds from hell" or "Devil Dogs." That's why this book is my "Devil Dog Diary."

"NEW YORK, SIR," I answered.

"IF YOU KEEP SCRATCHING, YOU'RE GONNA BE FROM CANCUN!" he roared back.

"YES SIR!" I shouted. Big as he is, I believe he really could have hit me hard enough to send me flying all the way to Mexico!

I kept score with Recruit Dion, and he told me a story about what his platoon once did to a recruit who kept screwing up. They wouldn't let him sleep. The first night they woke him up every 15 minutes, the second night every 10 minutes – until he finally got the picture and was squared away. I told Camden it sounded like a "kinder and gentler" blanket party for the 90s.

I saw Recruit Moreno later. We were recruited from the same office in New York. Moreno used to be with Platoon 1082, but he was transferred to 1086 and is now a squad leader. He told me there have been eight fights in 1086 since he's been there. Platoon 1086 is nasty.

This afternoon I was on Ammo work duty. I was picking up brass shells, and ran into two female recruits. They were very upset – sniffling and crying because there were only two weeks left before they were supposed to graduate, and they still hadn't qualified on the rifle range. No one becomes a Marine unless they qualify. "Every Marine a rifleman."

The women said that they actually *should* have qualified, but the girl doing the scoring cheated. They reported her, but it didn't help. Male recruits aren't really allowed to talk with the females, and typically they never even get a chance to, but I couldn't resist. I told them not to worry, that they'd qualify tomorrow and in two weeks they'd be laughing about it.

Another recruit told me "Shit, I'm supposed to be graduating this Friday, and I only scored a 189!" She missed qualifying by one friggin' point. In the back of my mind, I wondered how I would handle that kind of frustration, but I quickly blocked the thought out of my mind. There would be no "unq-ing," or not qualifying, in my future!

Today, I volunteered to get lunch chow for Recruit Nix and myself. After getting lunches and four juice bottles, I carried it all back – along with my rifle, which we always keep with us. "I am nothing without my rifle." As I walked, my rifle started slipping off my shoulder. I reached up to grab my sling and push it back. As I did, a hard-boiled egg flew out and hit the deck. As my (bad) luck would have it, the Company Commander was on the range, and of course he saw everything. This Marine Corps officer, who looks big enough and mean enough to be in the WWF, started letting me have it:

"RECRUIT!!" he screams at me, "WHAT THE HELL ARE YOU DOING! YOU'VE GOT NO DISCIPLINE, RECRUIT!"

"YES SIR," I answered. One way or another, Recruit Price is getting noticed by some pretty big guns.

Today my firing from both standing and kneeling positions sucked. I scored a 204 on the range anyway, but who's counting, right? Every *one* of us, in reality. I'm not worried about qualifying any more – I know I'm good enough. Now I'm just worried about getting an expert ranking. Speaking of expert, after two days of practice, we pushed that friggin' tower like a bunch of expert crazy men today. The trick is to get off to a good start together as a team and keep your momentum going. We were really smoking it down the runway.

It's Wednesday – but we're not going to be given haircuts this week because we're on the range. I know I'm changing now – I almost miss getting that cut. It makes me feel like a real military man. Oh well, we'll get haircuts next week. During Rifle Range days they keep you so busy every single second of the day that the time seems to just fly by. Fairly soon, 1082 will be back home at 1st Battalion, and it'll be like we never left.

Every night after shooting, we meet with PMI Cpl. Stevens. He's cool as hell. When we aren't talking about shooting, he tells us about BWT (Basic Warrior Training). Tonight he told us that we'd meet up with some 50-pound raccoons out there and that they were so big, just one of them could take out Recruit Camden. The guy only weighs about 125, so I don't know if he was kidding or not!

Then a recruit asked about sniper school. Our PMI gave him a mean look and said "Hell, who'd want to go to sniper school? You've got to sit in a hole in the ground for four straight days waiting to pop somebody. You can't move out of that hole – you've got to piss, shit

I don't know the actual height and weight of SDI Bixby, but as you can tell from this drawing of him I made in bootcamp, he seemed like he was seven feet tall and could easily bench press a tank.

and eat right in that same friggin' hole. No thank you!" Excellent point... noted, I thought to myself.

THURSDAY, APRIL 20: TD-27

After breakfast this morning, DI Parks was in a good mood – that is, until he saw a recruit from 1086 come out of chow smiling. I'm not sure about the other branches of the service, but on Parris Island, smiling recruits are not going to be smiling for very long. Recruits must maintain their military bearing at all times.

Parks was all over him – he did something that's rarely done. He ordered the recruit to walk through our platoon formation, rather than around it, or "break ranks." I'm not sure we would have let even a four-star General do that, and the recruit didn't want to, but orders are orders. So, he half-heartedly stepped in.

We jumped him so quick we were like a pack of wild, hungry dogs. We didn't hurt him or anything, but I guarantee he will not be smiling again anytime soon.

Today was our official Pre-Qual Day at the range, the last time to shoot the course, before the real deal. Somehow, I was switched from 5th relay to 1st relay this morning, so instead of being the last to shoot in the afternoon, I was now the first to shoot in the morning. At first I convinced myself it was no big deal – there would be less wind, easier to concentrate – but I was a little nervous. After shooting at the same time all week, was I now getting put out of rhythm?

When the range went hot, I was feeling good. I thought I'd bang out an expert score. I found a nice, tight sitting position and concentrated on nothing but the black of the bull. But unfortunately for me, I hadn't made the proper adjustments on my weapon before firing. A total freaking boot mistake, and it cost me dearly. The 200-yard slow fire, where you can "make your money" really kicked my ass. All my shots were hitting high, way high.

What the hell was I doing wrong? It didn't hit me until I was done with the slow fire and sitting on the scoring box. The aperture was wrong, and I had set my dope sight totally wrong – instead of 8/3-2, I was the other 8/3, the last setting from yesterday's round of firing from the 500-yard line. In other words, instead of setting my weapon to hit a target at just under 300 meters, I was set for a target at 500 meters. *Whoops*!

Needless to say I felt like a total moron. I recorded 44 out of 75 points – a total disgrace in my eyes. My shooting coach, Cpl. Robles, pretty much saw it the same way as he went off on me. "PRICE! HOW MANY TIMES DO I HAVE TO TELL YOU! WHAT THE HELL'S WRONG WITH YOU? DO YOU *WANT* TO FAIL?"

"NO SIR!"

"THEN GET WITH THE PROGRAM, RECRUIT!"

He was right, and I knew it. I totally lost my bearing. To make matters worse, at the 300-yard line, while marking my shots in my data book, I forgot to engage my weapon's safety. Coach Robles was all over me. "ARE YOU TRYING TO PISS ME OFF?? HAVE YOU LEARNED ANYTHING AT ALL THIS WEEK, OR AM I OUT HERE FOR MY HEALTH?!??

All I could muster was a pathetic "No, Sir," as he grabbed my book and red inked it with a safety violation warning. At this point, I could actually feel myself wanting to cry. Talk about frustration, I was having a complete meltdown. I was mad and angry with my coach, but really I was mad at myself for letting the range get the best of me. I was still pretty upset when a female sergeant saw me. I was expecting her to make me sink even lower, when instead of yelling at me some more, she calmed me down, motherly style.

"It's no big deal," she told me, "It's only PRE-qualifying. It's a good thing you made those mistakes today – now you won't make them tomorrow."

I had to agree. I had made mistakes. I expected shooting and qualifying to be easy, but now I knew it would take some hard work and practice. I made the worst mistake an infantryman can make, I had become overly complacent. Well, the truckload of humble pie I ate today will take care of that problem – tomorrow I'm going to do everything in my power to make things different.

After all that turmoil, I still managed to qualify, though it was by the skin of my teeth. Six recruits came up a little short on their pre-qual, including Recruit Lugo who missed it by one lousy point. He had been complaining about problems with his coach all week, so when they went off to the head for a "private discussion," I could only hope he wouldn't do anything stupid. Luckily, before anyone's manhood was put to the test any further that day, our Senior was in the right place at the right time, and with a snap of his fingers and a couple of choice words, Lugo was back in formation.

Tomorrow is the big day – Qualification for real. Marksmanship is the main skill of a good Marine, the basic core of the Corps. I'm going to focus my life into those targets and try for 39 minutes of perfect sight alignment, perfect sight picture, smooth trigger control and a correct natural respiratory pause. I WILL DO IT!

FRIDAY, APRIL 21: TD-28

Today was the day of reckoning. Did 1082 conquer the world? Unfortunately, we did not. Another platoon, 1080, won both best series and best company on the range. We had three recruits go unqualified, or "unq-sperts," as they're called, including Recruits Medina, Camden and Shales. DI Parks was pissed the hell off.

"I'M GOING TO MAKE YOUR FRIGGIN' HEAD EXPLODE!" he screamed at Shales.

And for a minute, I thought we were literally going to see Shales' head explode like an over-pumped balloon. The terrified look on Shales' face was crazy. Shales was screaming so loud, I thought he was going to die. All three unq-sperts from 1082 had to pack their trash up to meet later with another platoon, first thing in the morning, for a week, to try to qualify with them. If they can, they link back up with us, if not, they're history.

But on to the better news – Recruit Price qualified! Good to go! Unfortunately though, I only shot a 206 – qualified, but not expert. I screwed up big time during my standing shots. As I brought my rifle down to the target, nice and slow, my breathing was under control, but I flaked out. I accidentally pulled the trigger way, way, WAY too early – before I was even close to the target. My weapon was still at a 45-degree angle. The maximum range of the M16A2 is 3534 meters.

My "projectile" must have gone that far and then some. It probably landed in the Atlantic Ocean somewhere.

Afterward, I was so depressed and preoccupied by my score, I left my butt-pack, (a piece of gear), on the rifle range. Recruit Lugo picked it up, but instead of just giving it directly to me, he stupidly waited until we got back to the barracks. As if I didn't feel shitty enough, Lugo goes and tells DI Parks that he has it. Parks took it from him, then threw it down the hallway to me. I caught it and said, "THANK YOU!" forgetting to add "SIR." Well, that was it.

"COME HERE PRICE," he screams at me.

I ran down the hallway as fast as I could, and the damn floor was so slippery I started sliding. Parks saw it happening, and deliberately stepped into my path, knowing I'd hit him. Of course, I did. Aww shit.

"I *KNOW* YOU DIDN'T JUST HIT ME," he roars.

I yelled as loud as I possibly could "NO SIR!"

"YES YOU DID!" he answers.

We're supposed to keep arm's length away from the DIs at all times, so I started backing away from him. He grabbed me by the collar and began squeezing.

"PRICE, I'M SICK OF YOUR ATTITUDE!"

"YES SIR," I yelled as he squeezed his grip on my blouse.

"YOU BETTER GET SQUARED AWAY REAL QUICK!"

"YES SIR"

"NOW GET OUT OF MY SIGHT!"

"YES SIR!"

I raced back to my rack. Thanks a lot, Recruit Lugo. I was a little unnerved, but I was so depressed about failing to qualify as an expert, that I really couldn't think of anything else.

SATURDAY, APRIL 22: TD-29

It's 0200. We all got up two hours early to pack our sea bags so we could be ready right at wake-up for the 10-mile hump back to 1st Recruit Battalion – home. It's not really ten miles away from the rifle range, but they run you all over the friggin' place just to make it longer. They call it the "Tour of Parris Island." It was a real trip banging around in the complete darkness, trying to pack. It's a miracle DI Wight didn't hear us.

When the lights came on, Shales yelled, "RECRUIT SHALES REQUESTS PERMISSION TO SPEAK TO THE DRILL INSTRUCTOR!"

"GO AWAY SHALES, GO AWAY" was his reply. Unfortunately, he and the two others who unqed *did* go away. They were obviously mad at him for unqing on the range. For one thing, it makes our instructors look like they didn't do a good enough job teaching us to shoot. But what must really irk them, as it did all of us, was that Shales was qualifying all week. But come Qual day, he got so nervous he couldn't perform.

When it comes down to it, if a Marine cannot be at ease with his weapon when it counts, people will die. Plain and simple. So, whatever punishment is given to Shales, and recruits like him, is absolutely essential. It may help save lives, down the road.

Overall, we got a 94 percent rifle qualification rate, for a dismal third place finish. However, since we did do well *enough*, instead of the yellow flag with red numbers, we now march behind a red flag with yellow numbers. This may not seem like a big deal, but what it signifies is that we are on our way to the Third Phase, the final chapter of boot camp.

We hit the trail to DI Wight screaming BWT knowledge, which he made us repeat over and over about 200 times. On top of the 90-degree weather, and carrying all our gear in ALICE packs that seem to weigh as much as we do, we had to scream our Marine Corps knowledge at the top of our lungs. When it was SDI Bixby's turn to lead us, he found a way to motivate us, like he always does. We sang songs like, "Yellow Ribbon in Her Hair," "Sipping Bourbon Through a Straw," and "Inches." Our favorite was "Inches," which is about getting your belly up close to a woman's. OOH-RAH!

When we finally got back to the 1st Battalion barracks, Series Commander Capt. Dill inspected us for blisters and injuries. The Marines really are serious about "troop welfare." After inspection, we changed out of our sweat-soaked cammies and got weighed. I've lost 18 pounds! That's about three pounds a week – only 18 more to go. I can't tell you what an ego booster that was. It almost made me forget about my piss-poor rifle qual.

Next we had a "Corps Values" meeting with Bixby, which we do about once a week. Bixby makes up scenarios, and we have to tell him what we'd do in different situations. This teaches us about honor, commitment and courage. It sounds corny, but I actually get a lot out of it. I know that I've changed physically since I got to Parris Island, but I also know I have to change inside as well, and these meetings really teach me a lot.

Tonight is our last nine-hour sleep period. Tomorrow is "God Day," and possibly our last four-hour free-time period before BWT (Basic Warrior Training). Phase Two is over!

This statue on Parris Island commemorates Marines raising the flag on Iwo Jima's Mount Suribachi during World War II.

Recruits line up for chow in the Parris Island Mess Hall.

PHASE THREE

SUNDAY, APRIL 23 - MESS & MAINTENANCE WEEK

Officially, "Mess and Maintenance week" is not the true start of third phase, but since we performed so well, by qualifying enough recruits, our DIs were able to let us unfurl the yellow flag in place of the previous red one. The yellow flag lets the rest of the island know that we aren't boots just off the bus. After this week, there's Administrative Week, and then BWT or Basic Warrior Training. Throw in Final Drill, a bunch of inspections, tests and a whole lot of pain and we are basically done. But I think I am getting way ahead of myself.

I spent my four hours of free time period writing letters, cleaning my footlocker, ironing my uniforms, and working out. I can't believe how much weight I've lost, how neat my clothes are, and how good I'm looking in general. It doesn't seem like me anymore. Maybe it isn't.

I also polished my boots. Recruit O'Donnell pissed me off – he borrowed my can of polish, used more than half of it, then gave it back to me and said, "I only used a little!" For a minute I thought I was going to kill him. Then I realized it wasn't worth it. I'm beginning to realize that it's not the major things that piss me off. It is all the *little* things, combined, that make me go nuts!

I didn't get to go to church today. Too much trash to do. Third Phase is here. SDI Bixby told us this morning, "IT'S ALL DOWN HILL FROM HERE, BUT FOR SOME IT WILL BE ALL UPHILL!" I agree – but not for Recruit Price. I'm also trying to help other recruits from 1082. Today I gave Recruit Chidester a pep talk to help him stay motivated. It seems that even though he was able to call his girlfriend on the phone, she's still not handling their separation too well.

Sometimes it's hard for couples to understand that 12 weeks is really not that long. If they can just keep their eyes on the prize, everything will be all right. If your girlfriend wants to hug a rock-hard Marine stud, three months is a short time to wait. I guess some recruits come to me because they know I took a couple of psychology classes in college, and they know I'm a good listener. It makes me feel good to help them out when I can.

After free time ended, the Senior came out of the hut and read off our assignments. We came in 3rd out of six platoons at the rifle range. Two platoons got to pick their duty before us, as their reward for performing well on the range. So, as we had already figured, the majority of us got stuck in the mess hall. Five lucky recruits from Platoon 1082 got to work in the recycling department, and a couple worked as runners for the Company Police Sergeant. I knew where I was heading before my name was called.

So the rest of us fell out on the hardball and proceeded to march to 2nd Battalion Chow Hall to begin Mess and Maintenance duty. As we marched the 1/2-mile to the chow hall, our SDI called a cadence to the rhythm of the Marine Hymn. I thought, maybe this might not be so bad. Upon arrival, the mess hall certainly lived up to its name. The place was a mess all right – after a bunch of hungry recruits get through eating, mess halls looks like a bomb hit them. First order of duty was to assign everyone jobs for the week. The first position is called the Office Recruit. The sergeant from the chow hall asked, "WHO'S A NERDY MOTHERF'ER?"

Everyone started chanting "PRICE, PRICE, PRICE!" At first, I was pissed because they were calling me a nerd, but then I learned that in USMC lingo, nerdy is just another way of calling you smart. I thought it was cool to find out that my fellow recruits consider me intelligent. The "Office" job is mostly paperwork, which I don't mind. I did want to learn how to cook some of the trash they serve us, though.

Other jobs are Scullery (washing plates, cups, forks, etc.), Food Line (serving chow), Deck (making sure tables and floors are squared away), Pastry (serving treats), Juice (making sure the milk/soda/juice is good to go), Galley (helping the cooks with the slicing, dicing and swabbing), Salad (preparing the salad bar), Storeroom (helping keep goods in stock), and Guide (the guy who supervises the whole show). This week, our Guide was supposed to be Recruit Stillwell. I say "supposed to be" because Stillwell didn't last very long. While the sergeant was giving out positions, he spotted Stillwell picking his nose for all he was worth. The sergeant fired him on the spot – and it was brutal. He made him stand at attention, and screamed in his ear:

"REPEAT AFTER ME NASTY ONE: 'I AM A SNOT-PICKING, HEINOUS CREATURE!'"

"THIS RECRUIT IS A SNOT-PICKING, HEINOUS CREATURE!"

"YOU'RE FIRED! SAY IT, STILLWELL!"

"SIR, I AM FIRED SIR!" Stillwell repeated.

The sergeant then turned on us, and explained that he takes great pride in serving Marines and Marines-to-be, and "NO ONE – NO ONE – WILL GIVE MY CHOW HALL A BAD FRIGGIN' NAME!! OH, AND BY THE WAY, 'OFFICE!!'"

"YES, SIR" I responded.

"I WANT YOU TO PLACE STILLWELL ON GARBAGE DETAIL, UNTIL FURTHER NOTICE."

"AYE SIR," I said as I thought, wow, this guy means business. At first, I thought he was being hard on Stillwell, but then I could feel the pride in his voice. I saw that he, too, had the fire and commitment I'm searching for.

We were then given our prison-like white uniforms for the week. After busting our asses all day getting the place ready to serve chow, we were surprised to notice that the day was already over. We arrived back at the barracks to find the other recruits already sitting there, doing nothing, but we were so tired all we could think about was sleep.

MONDAY, APRIL 24 MESS & MAINTENANCE WEEK

At 0300, SDI Bixby stormed into the squad bay without warning.

"GET UP! GET UP! OUT OF THOSE RACKS! WAKE UP YOUR STINKIN' BODIES!!"

I got used to getting up at 0500 a long time ago – but getting up *two hours earlier* was a real trip. Boy, did wake-up arrive quickly. It was the first time in a long time that I didn't remember where I was. It took me a few seconds just to realize that I was even alive.

We put on our nasty little white uniforms and headed to the 2nd Battalion chow hall. When we first came to Parris Island it was every man for himself, but now we've learned how to act as a team. We're working together pretty well – even when making and serving food. Everyone is doing his part, with no complaints.

I saw a recruit today at lunch chow. He seemed down, so I gave him a nice loud, "STAY MOTIVATED, RECRUIT! Time flies while you're here!" His reply to me was "Ten days to go Recruit!" I got a big dopey grin on my face – and, of course, DI Parks just happened to see me. Our DIs are somewhat scarce during M&M week, and Parks has hardly showed his face. However, the second I smiled, there he was, with a look that could kill. You can't get away with much here.

"PRICE! YOU HAD BETTER GET THAT STUPID LOOK OFF YOUR FRIGGIN" FACE! FOLLOW ME OUTSIDE!" he screamed in my face. Aww, shit!

I followed him as he walked outside. On the way, he slipped and almost busted his ass! I didn't even think of laughing, because I knew he'd give it to me twice as hard for losing my bearing, *and* laughing at him almost falling. I was right.

When we got outside, he let me have it. He got right in my face and grabbed me by the blouse with a clenched fist. I thought shit, he's really gonna do it this time. Well, I probably deserve it for being way too loose. He stopped about two inches from my face and delivered a message that I will never forget.

"I WILL NEVER BE EMBARRASSED BY YOU IN THIS STINKIN' CHOW HALL AGAIN!"

"YES SIR!" I roared at the top of my lungs.

"DO YOU HEAR ME, PRICE?"

"YES SIR!" If I had yelled any louder my head would've exploded.

"ONE OF THESE DAYS, MEN'S LIVES WILL BE IN YOUR HANDS! DO YOU THINK THEY'RE GONNA LISTEN TO SOME PUNK-ASS KID THAT JUST WANTS TO SMOKE AND JOKE ALL DAY?!?!"

"NO SIR, NO SIR!!"

"Today during lunch, we played a good joke on Recruit Stillwell. He was taking a crap and taking his sweet old time about it. So we decided to 'motivate' him..

This was the second time he had grabbed me, but this time I really felt like he was guiding me with his own personal advice. Before I came to Parris Island this would have totally enraged me, but my attitude has changed since I came here. Now it doesn't bother me that he grabbed me like that, because I know that if he only yelled at me, the message would not hit home.

I must learn to maintain my military bearing at all times – that's just part of being a good Marine. And if it takes being grabbed, choked, punched to make me remember that, then let them do what it takes. Some may find this type of training excessive, but the Marine Corps is a no-nonsense business. If you are not prepared to go all the way – stay home.

Later that evening, the Master Gunnery Sergeant in charge of the chow hall sat us all down for a talk about the rest of the week to come. Among other valuable points of advice, this one stood out in my mind: he said, "DON'T EVER MAKE SOMEBODY TELL YOU TO DO SOMETHING THAT YOU *KNOW* NEEDS TO GET DONE ANYWAY."

This is a lesson I have to learn – and I WILL learn it.

TUESDAY, APRIL 25 MESS & MAINTENANCE WEEK

We were awakened at 0400 and began the march to the "Mess" right away. It was cold as hell, so we stepped it out really quick. DI Parks was with us, and even he was cold. As we marched, he chuckled and said, "I BET YOU RECRUITS FEEL LIKE IT'S TIME TO MAKE THE DOUGHNUTS!" We all remembered the Dunkin' Doughnuts commercial with that pathetic fat guy "makin' the doughnuts," and laughed.

Then we ate breakfast – they really feed us like champs during M & M week. I think I've gained back a pound already! During chow, Parks was a one-man typhoon. He busted on everyone! He called Recruit Burton and Recruit Rivera, Potato Head #1 and #2, and imitated Recruit Donner's grizzly voice to a "T." Walking up and down the aisle, he shouted, "SOME OF US ARE GONNA GET SOME FROM SUZIE AT GRADUATION, AREN'T WE? AND THEN, SOME OF US ARE GOING TO GET A **BOOT** UP OUR ASS AT GRADUATION."

Then he came right up to me, staring at me with those wild eyes, and whispers in my ear, "ISN'T THAT RIGHT, PRICE?"

"YES SIR!" I answered automatically, only cracking a smile after he turned his back.

Today during lunch, we played a good joke on Recruit Stillwell. He was taking a crap and taking his sweet old time about it. So we decided to 'motivate' him. Recruits Palarino and Davis pretended to be DIs calling him as we all waited outside the head's door.

"STILLWELL! GET YOUR SORRY ASS OUT HERE DOUBLE-TIME!"

"MOVE, MOVE, MOVE, YOU'RE DONE SHITTIN! DONE, DONE!"

Stillwell was frantic. He came running out of the shitter so fast, that he probably forgot to wipe his ass. It was a riot.

"SIR, RECRUIT STILLWELL REPORTING AS ORDERED, SIR!" When Stillwell finally saw us all standing there cracking up, he smiled, gave us the finger, and returned to the stall.

After lunch, I asked a female sergeant if she thought Platoon 1082 was doing a good job at working the chow hall.

"DON'T BE A KISS-ASS, RECRUIT!" she replied loudly. Meanwhile, she's probably sucking up to every DI in the place, but she was right. What did I really want to hear? She can be a real sweet lady when she wants to be, and one tough Marine when she wants to be. I was mad at first, but I've noticed that no one really likes her – except when they want food from her, that is.

At dinner I made the menu sign, saying what was for chow, along with a little sign to let everyone know who was *serving* their grub. It said, "PLATOON 1082 Proud to serve, Ready to fight!" (this is the motto for the East Coast MEPS). I finished by writing the calorie count of what was being served, and the name of the Marine who made the chow. While everyone was getting in line for chow, I started to prepare hot tray meals to get ahead of the rush. These are meals for Marines who are not able to come to chow for different reasons – sick or broken, on duty, etc. – or for DIs who are eating on the run.

Everyone was formed for chow, and I got in line last. I was dead tired, my mind was wandering a bit, and that's when DI Parks appeared out of nowhere. I hear, "PRICE!! CURL YOU STINKIN' FINGERS." It is necessary to walk at all times with your fists clenched, and needless to say, I was the only one caught slipping, and Parks noticed right away. It's Third Phase now, and I really should know better, but my face must have said, "God, I've busted my ass all day, can't I get a freaking break?" I could see the answer to that question in his eyes: I think he was ready to kill me. He put his hands behind his back and stuck his chin out at me. He then began laying into me ultra-thick.

"GO AHEAD, PRICE HIT ME! GO AHEAD! THE FIRST SHOT IS YOURS – THE REST ARE MINE! GO AHEAD – DO IT!"

I wanted to, but of course hitting him was not an option. I just said, "SIR, THIS RECRUIT DOESN'T THINK THAT WOULD BE SUCH A GOOD IDEA, SIR!"

This little moment in time seemed to last forever as he kept begging me to take a swing. When it was all over, I was a bit rattled, not really feeling as hungry as I had been a minute ago, but I tried to get the message he was sending to me. I understand now that I must think and behave like a Marine *all the time.* Not just when I'm being "watched," but 24 hours a day, 7 days a week, 52 weeks a year, and for the next four years.

What I did wasn't really so bad, but it was incorrect. If Parks sees it as a problem now, then somebody will definitely see it as a problem after I graduate. I've got to develop the correct attitude here and now, or it will come back to haunt me later. A Marine without discipline is not a Marine. I know that now. Each day I'm getting stronger, wiser, and more focused.

When I came back from dinner, I was surprised to find that Recruit Martin had spit-shined my boots while I was gone. He did a great job, and it was a genuinely nice thing to do. After my run-in with Parks, that really brightened my day. Just one example of how we're all pulling together as a team. OOH-RAH!

WEDNESDAY, APRIL 26 - MESS & MAINTENANCE WEEK

Another exhausting day of M&M. Today Sgt. Cummings ordered me to write the menu – he handed me a grease-stick and told me to repeat after him:

"THIS IS MY GREASE STICK. THERE ARE MANY OTHERS LIKE IT, BUT THIS ONE IS MINE. LOSE IT AND I'LL KICK YOUR ASS!"

I saw Recruit Ruiz today at lunch – he's the recruit who got dropped after IST (Initial Strength Test) right in the beginning and sent to PCP (Physical Conditioning Platoon). He has yet to start Training Day 1. But despite this, he was still in an awesome mood. He actually told *me* to stay motivated. Here is a guy who would be right along with us, if only his recruiter had done a better job of insuring that Ruiz was ready physically. Instead, Ruiz was now six weeks behind, and here he was telling *me* to stay motivated! I give him a world of credit, and then some. He's an inspiration. Every time I get down, I'll remember his motivation for encouragement.

After making about 100 hot trays for lunch, I stopped for a minute to rest. I took off my portholes (glasses) and was rubbing my eyes when I heard someone calling for me. I couldn't see who it was without my portholes, so I snapped to attention and ran up to the DI.

"RECRUIT PRICE REPORTING AS ORDERED, SIR!"

"RECRUIT, PUT ON YOUR PORTHOLES!"

I did, and then recognized the DI. It was Tim McMahon, an old neighbor of mine! He'd joined up about eight years before I did, and had gone to DI school. Man, did they work him over. He was awesome. And what a sight for sore eyes. He was done and on his way home. His tour of duty on the Island was over, but he knew I was there and made it a point to see me before he left. We talked for about 15 minutes – he gave me some good advice on how to survive the rest of Basic.

"Do you have any vicious Recruits?" he wanted to know.

"Not really," I told him. It felt strange not addressing a DI as SIR, but this was my old buddy who I grew up playing basketball, football, and stickball (you name it) with. He told me DIs love vicious recruits and then he was gone, off to his next position of duty and adventure. I was sad to see him go, but I rejoined my platoon, which was already eating. I was totally pumped.

I should mention that the chow is actually pretty good. Some recruits don't like it too much, but having tasted college food, I know better. Also, normally, recruits get only a pre-set amount of every dish served, but

A self-portrait of Recruit Price, drawn on the back of a letter, complete with Eagle, Globe and Anchor emblem on my cover and "BC" goggles (BC = Birth Control, because they make women laugh at you).

during M & M week, we're getting all the food we can eat, and then some! Personally, I stocked up big time on yogurt and fruit.

One nickname for Marines is "Devil Dogs," which is why this book is called *"Devil Dog Diary."* Recruits are sometimes called "Devil Pups," so tonight's dinner sign said, "Blood-thirsty, Training-hungry Devil Pups!"

Recruit Medina finally made it back from the rifle range. He qualified with a 197. Recruit Shales also came back. Camden is the last from 1082 who still hasn't qualified. Rumor has it he can't hit the side of a barn. He has until this Friday to qualify. If he doesn't, then it's good-bye Camden. For the record, once you go "unq," it doesn't matter if you score a perfect 250, your score goes down in the books as 190, or marksman.

Marching back from the chow hall, DI noticed we were really dogging it, so he made us march double-time. I don't know how I made it without dropping – but I did. I never thought I could get up so early, do so much, and still have enough energy left to march double-time and not collapse. The Marines have really shown me that the limits I used to apply to myself were way too confining. They're working me like I've never worked before, and have me doing things I never would have believed. I've never been so tired in my life, but it feels great.

Wednesday is usually our weekly haircut day – but today is the sixteenth day that Platoon 1082 has gone without haircuts. There just wasn't enough time during Rifle Range or M & M. Our hair has grown in a lot from our usual recruit cuts. My head is starting to look like a Chia pet, with hair sticking out all over the place.

Still, my hair is way shorter than any messed-up civilian haircut I ever had, which leads me to the question: Why do I feel like a hippie? Answer: Because Recruit Price is taking pride in his appearance. Recruit Price is thinking like a Marine.

Mess Hall duty is more hectic and tiring than anything is. We have to get up so early every morning, and we're so friggin' busy all day that the time speeds by. The whole day is like a blur. Since the start of the week, we've been having some minor incidents with some of the 'saltier' platoons.

So when I got out of my rack this morning, I had a funny feeling we were going to have more problems today – and boy was I right. During breakfast, Recruit Lish, who happens to be one of our tougher "devil pups," was serving pastry to some Third Phase Recruits from 2nd Battalion, who were acting cocky as hell. Instead of the usual "Pastry, Recruit" this guy says, "Give me the pastry, MF."

"What did you call me?" Lish asked. "You heard me, a-hole." Lish had already heard enough, so he stepped around the counter to confront the troublemaker. Suddenly, somebody pushed him hard in the back. Lish spun around to the recruit who did it and clocked him in the face knocking him right on his ass. DI Wight tried to grab Lish, but Lish didn't know who was grabbing him. Lish threw Wight off him like he was a rag doll.

Before I could take two steps to help, DIs were all over Lish. They dragged him to a wall, pressed him up against it, nose-first, and started screaming at him like you wouldn't believe. Meanwhile, my veins were pumping and my fists were tight – but I didn't interfere. It's amazing how my training took over. If I had been closer, I know I would have done anything I could have to help my platoon mate.

Lish spent the rest of the morning in the Master Sergeant's office, cooling off and explaining his side of the story. End result: Lish was no longer serving pastry. He ended up way out of sight, washing pots in the potshack, then he had to polish all the platoon's inspection buckles during the next three nights on his free time. Those other recruits finally started behaving themselves too. All in all, the story got around and platoons started showing servers the proper respect.

At lunch I drew pictures on some of 1082's Mess covers – nasty little white paper hats – and they were a big hit. Before I knew it everybody wanted one. SDI Bixby thought they were funny, but told me not to get too crazy with them. Hope he's not pissed at me. I was told later that several compliments were given – our Series Commander even noticed Recruit Mulroy's. He's about as Irish as they come, so I drew the Lucky Charms' Leprechaun on his, complete with diamonds, stars, and whatever the hell else was on the box. Clovers?

Tonight in the squad bay, our Senior told us about his visit to the third-phase recruits' DI's house. He was in charge of the recruit who started the fight. Our Senior said he could hear their platoon being attacked by their DIs for the trash they pulled at breakfast before he even went inside.

They were drenched in sweat and screaming so loud that he thought the squad bay roof would pop off. Their DIs had them tearing their mattresses apart – to the springs. They deserve the punishment they're getting, but I feel sorry for the recruits who had nothing to do with it. They didn't deserve that torture, but they are a unit – and for better or worse, they're in it together.

At this point in Third Phase, it's harder to put the fear of God into us, like they could in the very beginning. We even imitate our DI's in chow hall, and I must admit, I'm guilty too. This is partially a result of DI's having a lot of their power taken away from them in recent years. They still abuse us for sure – that's their job – but it's not like it used to be, when they could do just about anything and get away with it. Sometimes I wish it were still like that, because some of these nasty recruits need a lot more punishment than they're getting.

I can understand the DI's frustrations – they're here to train Marines, not baby-sit. Either you get the most out of it, or you don't – it's your choice. But I know exactly what *I* want to do.

I got a package from Kimball today – he sent me a chocolate candy bar. Good to go! I was able to somehow sneak it by the DI to save for later – my mouth was watering all day just thinking about it. I could hardly wait to eat it. Usually the DI would notice food coming in the mail, but he must have been a little tired cause he let it slide. It'd be worse if it weren't M&M week.

They're suddenly feeding us like turkeys before Thanksgiving – or, I should say, recruits before BWT (Basic Warrior Training) – which is coming soon. I can't believe tomorrow is Friday.

FRIDAY, APRIL 28 - MESS & MAINTENANCE WEEK

Man did we get tired during M & M. Today when lunch was over, I asked Recruit Fowler "Was that dinner?" The best thing about it was getting to talk with the Marines assigned to Parris Island chow duty. I feel bad for some of them, because when you join up you don't expect to be spending your whole four years as a Marine in a nasty chow hall. We'll (hopefully) all be out of here soon, but they've got to stay and stay. For those who hate it, it's like a prison.

I saw Recruit Ruiz again. Monday he starts TD-1 with 3rd Battalion. He seemed so happy that I was happy for him – but I have learned to maintain my military bearing, and not to smile. Recruits have a sort of signal to each other instead. We flex the muscles in our cheeks, and that signals "Good to go!"

I signaled to him. He saw me and flexed back. I was really proud of his esprit de corps – I felt like a father watching his son grow up. He was no longer the confused and inconsistent boy I had shared a hotel room with way back at MEPS. PCP had him looking in the best shape of his life, and now he was good to go all the way.

SATURDAY, APRIL 29 - MESS & MAINTENANCE WEEK

The last day of M & M has finally arrived. No one can believe this week is almost over. No more bitching DIs from other platoons getting their rocks off by ragging on us. No more Diet Menus. No more cleaning up slop and stomping huge friggin' cockroaches (oops, I didn't say that). One thing I will miss, though, are the "designer covers," I drew for almost half of 1082. Here are some of the slogans I put on them:

"SOUND OFF LIKE YOU GOT A PEAR!" (With a little picture of a pear)

"BORN TO SCRUB POTSHACK!"

"SCULLERY – DANGER!" (Complete with skull & crossbones)

"THE LINE DOES IT BETTER!" (Serves chow that is!)

"SOUND OFF FOR BROWN COW!" (Chocolate milk)

The scullery and potshack recruits were awesome. They have to clean pots, pans, forks, spoon and trays, etc. – probably the nastiest jobs there were – yet, they were screaming with MOTIVATION the whole time. The scullery and potshack recruits had to be hating life, though. Those are some really nasty ass jobs. The Salad Recruits laid low and stuffed themselves full of fruit, while the Juice Recruits were harassed all week by Third Phase Recruits who think they're real Marines already. For me, Recruit Price, I just did my job, observing, making up hot trays and drawing covers by popular demand. I think even SDI Bixby was impressed with my work. He told Recruit Mulroy to make sure he kept the cover I drew for him.

Recruit Duvall met the platoon today. He juiced (told) us all about the hell of being in PCP (Physical Conditioning Platoon). "Man, it sucks so bad. You wake up at 0400, workout and PT like a dog all day, then rack out at 2000." He had everyone crapping their pants.

We lost Recruit Camden today. He was a good kid. He tried hard, but he just couldn't get that rifle trash down. He's been set back three friggin' weeks – and has to do Grass week all over. It must be weird having to join a whole new platoon. Good luck little guy – Recruit Price is pulling for you.

Since coming here, I've lost a lot of weight and my attitude has improved 100 percent. In just the last three days alone, I've done about 1500 push-ups and those were mostly on my own. Whenever I could get a free moment, I would go to my little hiding space in the chow hall and crank out 50 push-ups at a time.

M&M duty is one of the only times in boot camp when your DIs don't thrash you too much and there is no PT scheduled, so it is important to do some PT on your own. People are starting to notice the changes in me, too, which makes me feel pretty good. Tomorrow we introduce the next batch of recruits to their new M & M jobs – our old jobs – and then it's see ya later, chow hall.

SUNDAY, APRIL 30

No more M&M. I never thought I'd say it, but it feels good to get back into the old cammies again. Those white M & M uniforms were ridiculous. Now that it's over, I realize that I'm going to miss the people I worked with during week of M & M. When I get on-base liberty the day before Graduation, maybe I'll stop by and say hello.

I trained my "replacement" today. We were all so naive starting M&M; it was funny to be training somebody else to do it. We all sounded so wise and experienced. While I was training my replacement, I heard Springsteen's "Born To Run" on the radio. "We're gonna get to that place where we really wanna go, and we'll walk in the sun – but 'til then, tramps like us, baby we were born to run!" First time I've heard music in a long time. Awesome!

M&M seemed like hell at first – I couldn't see the point of Marines training to be cooks, but by the end of the week I could see the good effect it had on all of us. It really pulled us together as a team, and we needed that. I also got the first nickname I've ever had that doesn't have to do with partying or mischief. Because my SDI found out I took psychology classes in college, he always thinks I'm sort of "analyzing" everyone during my conversations, including him. So now he's got everyone calling me "The Doctor," or "Doc." I can't believe I'm being recognized like that. At first it made me feel awkward, but I'm starting to really like my new handle.

DI Parks is still up my ass. I passed by him at dinner, and I didn't *stop* when I said, "Good evening, Sir," which we have to say whenever we pass a superior. And since we're just nasty privates, everyone is our superior. I actually didn't see him, but with Parks it still made no difference, he still went wild.

"BOY, I'M GONNA JACK YOU UP!'

"YES SIR!" I shouted automatically.

"IT SEEMS I STILL NEED TO TEACH YOU SOME STINKING MANNERS!! WELL, I'M GONNA LOCK YOU ON LATER! YOU JUST STINKIN' STAND BY!" As he railed me, I could see him making fists. In a daze of "holy shit, I can't believe I'm getting my ass chewed in front of the entire chow hall," all I could see were his veins popping all the way from his hands, up his arms ending in his temples. He was fuming.

"YES SIR!" The best response I know to get out of a DI confrontation with the least amount of pain.

"NOW GET OUTTA HERE!"

"YES SIR!" (And was I outta there with a quickness!)

That little encounter may not seem like a big deal, but it messed up my whole dinner. Parks really knows how to get inside my head. As I ate my meal, with my stomach turning, all I could think of is when I would mess up again. If keeping us on edge is part of the job description, and I believe it is, Parks is doing his job extremely well.

As I write this, I just got off fire watch. It sucked, but like all fire watches, it ended. Next for us is Administration week – we take our official pictures in dress blue uniforms, do paperwork, make a PX call and trash like that. Tomorrow is TD-30 and our next haircut. It's about time.

MONDAY, MAY 1: TD-30 - ADMINISTRATION WEEK

The first day of Administration Week. Back to good old regular Training Days. OOH-RAH! We finally PTed in the morning – but they've upped the ante again. All exercise counts have been increased. It's harder for sure, but it's for our own good. We need to be strong.

Marching to the barbershop this afternoon, I think the whole platoon couldn't wait for a haircut. I can hardly remember hating those recruit cuts. Looking around at my fellow recruits' heads, I couldn't help but laugh to myself. It reminded me of one of those war movies where everyone comes out of the field with beards, except for us, it was our nasty heads. It's amazing how they change your mind about your hair.

Before we came to PI, we were just nasty civilians with our hair everywhere. Our hair styles represented who we were, and in a way what we believed in. Some recruits were used to hiding behind their hair, like they were hiding behind a tree. The Marines took all that hair away first thing, and with it, they took away our past, too. Nothing in our past seemed to matter anymore, because the USMC was starting us all over at square one. When they cut off our hair, they exposed all of us for exactly what we were inside. Our immaturity, lack of discipline and direction was put right out in the open for everyone – including us – to see. I rubbed my bald head as I got out of the barber chair, and instead of feeling weird, it felt right.

The Marines really are "The few, the proud," like the slogan says. They demand your utmost, and those who join have to accept the

"As I looked up into in the blue sky over Parris Island, I saw myself; I saw the whole world; I saw infinity..."

challenge of being put back in the starting blocks. They have something special even before they join, and the Corps refines it and develops it to the fullest. Simply meeting the requirements for graduation does NOT make you a Marine. That only comes from inside. To a large extent, the Marines don't *build* character – they *reveal* it.

This afternoon, during PT, something amazing happened to me. I was waiting to do crunches, lying flat on my back and looking straight up. I saw nothing but blue sky. But as I continued looking, I suddenly saw something else. I thought of how incredibly huge the sky is, and I suddenly felt as though all my limitations were being removed. I realized that since coming to Boot Camp, I had changed into a totally different person, free of all my old limits. I no longer had boundaries.

As I looked up into in the blue sky over Parris Island, I saw myself; I saw the whole world; I saw infinity. As surreal as this sounds, I know I will never look at an open sky again without remembering this moment.

TUESDAY, MAY 2: TD-31 - ADMINISTRATION WEEK

Another glorious day in the Marine Corps. Today we did PT at the Table and had a 3-mile run. My abs are killing me from the increased reps they added to our regular workout, but I'm not letting it get to me. Once again, I volunteered to move up to a faster run group. Man, is that trash hard!

The rest of the day, we prepared for the Series Commander's inspection on Saturday. We spit-shined our boots, ironed our cammies, and made our last PX call. A lot of Third-Phasers had been telling us that Administration Week was hell, and that we'd be living in the pit. They were right. After a week of Rifle and a week of M & M, your marching gets really rusty. Our drilling was really off today, but for some reason Bixby didn't pit us. Instead, he put this incredible guilt trip on us about pulling our heads out of our asses and getting our priorities straight. After he was done, I felt so bad I wished he *had* pitted us – we sure needed it.

Recruit Lish finally served out his punishment for the the Mess Hall Melee last week. Not so bad – a few hours of his free time was taken away, and he has to shine belt buckles instead. A small price to pay. Bixby tells us that we're soon going to have a new DI to "break in." That means we'll have *four* DIs. Somehow, I don't think we'll be breaking him in – far from it. Personally I was glad. We need some new blood around here to get us squared away. Some of our goons are getting a bit loose as of late.

WEDNESDAY, MAY 3: TD-32 - ADMINISTRATION WEEK

"THE PRIDE OF WEARING YOUR UNIFORM BEGINS HERE," the sign says. We received our first Service-Alpha uniforms today. What a great feeling. There were no mirrors, so I couldn't see myself, but everybody else looked great. (Being the handsome devil I am, I assumed I, too, was looking awesome). We also got our dog tags. What an amazing feeling to see them in my hands for the first time – I think I am really in the Marines. Good to go!

DI Wight had some fun with the hose this afternoon. He soaked the squad bay deck for about 20 minutes and then we had to clean it with our "skuzz brushes." Skuzzing that deck at full speed is some workout on the legs. Let me tell you, we don't need any more PT today.

Today, on the way to dinner chow, the sand fleas were out in full force and apparently were immune to our usual "Skin So Soft" bug repellent. The limited amount of swatting that we used to get away with when we had only one DI marching us will not fly so easily now. I was caught red-handed by our new DI, who had quietly started following the formation. After dinner, Recruit Price found himself in the pit for scratching his nose in formation. DI Wight let our new DI, Ojeda, pit me along with four other recruits who had screwed up.

Ojeda took us all outside for about 20 minutes – a long time as pit calls go, but not too bad. He tried to improve our physical condition and instill discipline in us at the same time by stopping every 3-4 minute to let us know what we did and why it was wrong. It sucked, yet I kind of liked it at the same time. DI Ojeda is a definite asset to 1082. When he let us go, we hauled ass back into the barracks dripping with sweat and sand everywhere. Ahh, the joys of Parris Island.

Inspection is only three days away. I'm dead tired, but I intend to pick it up anyway. BWT (Basic Warrior Training) is on the horizon.

About eight recruits still haven't made it up that rope. The clock is ticking. I got another amazing letter from Kirk tonight. He's never been in the military, but he seems to know exactly what I need to hear to help motivate me. I guess good friends can read each other's minds. He ordered me to call him by his last name from now on, just like us recruits – so from now on it's KIMBALL. Good to go! He's such a wiseass, but what best friend isn't?

THURSDAY, MAY 4: TD-33 - ADMINISTRATION WEEK

Today started at 0200 for me. 1st Recruit Battalion has pulled sentry battalion fire watch, and Recruit Price had to post guard number 3. So, instead of just making sure all is well in our own squad bay, we are now set to patrol 1st Battalion's area. All you do during fire watch is walk around for an hour and a half and make sure there's nothing out of order or "unusual" – and that, of course, would include fires. And naturally, you have to carry your rifle the whole time. *"I am nothing without my rifle."*

I relieved the recruit on fire watch before me, and at that time of night Parris Island looked like a ghost town. As I walked my designated perimeter, my mind started to wonder. I started practicing rifle movements while I marched to my own whispered cadence. It's amazing how many different ways you can invent to carry your rifle when no one's watching, or at least I thought no one was watching.

When I got to the end of the block, I was face-to-face with two hungry and rather ominous raccoons. To say the least, they scared the crap out of me, but luckily I scared them *more*, and they ran away. Other than that it was, "Nothing unusual to report for this recruit." Just a couple of killer raccoons and also a nervous, but huge possum.

Oh I almost forgot – I saw SDI Bixby's truck up-close for the first time. I was a little shocked to discover he smokes. Not just a little, but a shit load! It must kill him to not be able to smoke in our presence, because if he is allowed to, he never has. I also saw some cassette tapes he had, which included, of all things, the soundtrack to St. Elmo's Fire. HAH! Maybe Bixby *is* human.

After all was said and done, I found myself back in my BVDs and under the covers. It was already 0345, only one hour and change till reveille. All I remember was thinking, "great..." when all of a sudden... "WAKE UP YOUR STINKIN' BODY! GET UP! GET UP!"

Today DI Wight caught Recruit Butler sleeping after wake-up. Man did he go off! It was the most brutal quarter decking I ever saw. By the time Wight was done with him, Butler was moaning like a woman. It seems like your head just hits the pillow, and suddenly it's time to get up again. All part of their plan to keep us busy every second of the day.

This morning we PTed in our cammies, and for the first time, everyone made it up the rope. It looked like everyone, even Recruit Donner, was going to have a good day – then came a two-mile run. Look out!

DI Wight warned us ahead of time, "LISTEN UP MAGGOTS!! TODAY IS GOING TO BE A HOT ONE. YOU WILL BE DOING PT IN BOOTS AND UT'S (utilities or cammie bottoms). IT'S GOING TO BE HOTTER THAN TWO RATS F-ING IN A WOOL SOCK!" Boy, that sure sounds *hot*, I thought to myself. I'll have to remember that one. "SO START SUCKING DOWN WATER! OPEN UP YOUR CANTEENS AND BEGIN!"

We each guzzled down two canteens apiece, ran back to the head filled up two more, drained them and filled two more in reserve. Some guys began coughing up water and part of morning chow. Some tried to only fill their canteens half way, got caught, as we always are, and received some extra PT on the quarterdeck. To let the DI know we were done, we had to hold the canteen upside-down over our grapes (heads).

Two miles equals six laps around the track, and after about three laps some of 1082s recruits started dropping like flies. First to start losing it was a recruit from another platoon in the follow series. When Donner, who was running in front of me, saw he wouldn't be the first, he started to drop.

"DONNER!" I yelled at him, "DON'T DO IT... DON'T DO IT!!"

He managed to run another 100 yards, but then couldn't go on. Instead of running to the side of the track, he just instantly dropped to the deck right in front of me. To me it seemed like he was faking a leg injury. The old "OOOH there goes my ankle" trick or the "Damn, gotta tie my shoelaces." Because they're always weighing us, we all know each other's weight by heart. Donner weighs 212 pounds and is about

"START SUCKING WATER! OPEN UP YOUR CANTEENS AND BEGIN!"

6'5". When he dropped, I almost got taken out with him. He screws up so much, I can't believe he's still with us. I'm sorry, but if he graduates, that trash just isn't right. The rest of us had to work too damn hard to earn the title of Marine to just give it away to a nasty, weak recruit like him.

Next, we drilled. Two DIs from Platoon 1081, named Gaita and Hansen, came over to help supervise our platoon. Actually, it was more like they were sizing us up. They were really a pisser. They like to single recruits out and bust on them – they even got me. Gaita claimed I was holding the bayonet stud on my rifle with my pinky, something I never do. It's a way of cheating when holding your weapon at "TRAIL ARMS." I will admit that my finger was touching it, but in no way was I supporting the weapon illegally. That little tidbit of truth did not seem to matter much to DI Gaita. He went crazy on me.

"HEY RECRUIT PRICE, YOU JUST WANT TO HOLD YOUR WEAPON WITH YOUR LITTLE PINKY, LIKE A LITTLE GIRL!!" He seemed serious.

"NO SIR," I responded, feeling accused of something I didn't do. That's when things started to get out of hand.

"ARE YOU IN 4TH BATTALION, PRICE?" (The female battalion)

"NO SIR!" He was practically touching my face, trying to make me lose my bearing. I was prepared not to budge.

"ARE YOU A LAZY RECRUIT?"

"NO SIR!"

"YES YOU ARE!"

"NO SIR!"

"ARE YOU CALLING ME A LIAR? YOU'RE LAZY!"

"NO SIR!"

Then DI Hansen got in the act. The two of them were screaming in my ears, saying it and spraying it right in my face. They were a two-man circus. "WHO DO YOU THINK YOU ARE?? YOU NASTY, NO DISCIPLINED LITTLE MAGGOT!" You get the idea. Finally, Hansen yells, "IF I SAY THE SKY IS RED, IT'S RED! IS IT RED?" I decided this was my cue to roger up.

"SIR, YES SIR!" I screamed out. They finally left me alone.

Later we turned in our shirts – many in 1082 have been promoted to Private First Class and those who did got their stripe sewn on. I received a promotion for encouraging one of my high school friends to join the Marines. Since he joined up, I get an automatic promotion to PFC. My credits from college qualified me too. This means an increase in pay, and it puts me that much closer to picking up the next highest rank, Lance Corporal. Good to go! But again, I'm getting ahead of myself. I haven't even graduated yet!

One day to inspection. It seems like for every "Irish Pennant" (loose thread) I cut off my cammies, another two appear. From top to bottom, everything's got to be perfect. Good thing I've finally learned how to spit-shine my boots properly. Tomorrow we get our pictures taken in our dress blue uniforms!

FRIDAY, MAY 5: TD-34 - ADMINISTRATION WEEK

After our usual "gentle" wake-up, we marched to chow and then did some morning drill. Coming back home, we passed by the parade deck and saw another series of platoons graduating. It was awesome seeing those newly-minted Marines marching around, and imagining ourselves on that day. When we got back to the squad bay with the DI in his "house," or office, several recruits couldn't stop looking out the portholes (windows) at the ceremony.

Of course, when one too many of us joined the mob, out came our DI – none too happy. One second we were picturing ourselves on the parade deck, the next we were on the quarterdeck, getting the life thrashed out of us. We would have been out in the hot, sandy pit, had there not been hundreds of families that would have seen us. Four weeks away, Platoon 1082 cannot wait for graduation! The saying, "So close, yet so far," comes to mind.

After that, we got our official "dress-blues" picture taken. We discovered that we don't get to wear *real* dress blues, just something called "mock" dress blues – the cover (hat) and the top half of the jacket that you see in the picture are real, but the jacket ends at your stomach. It's like a cutoff T-shirt. They brush you off so there's not a speck of lint on your jacket, and then you're hustled in front of a

Recruit Price in the legendary Marine Dress Blues uniform... sort of. To expedite the photographing of 300 recruits in dress blues, this is only a "simulated" uniform. The actual blouse only extends halfway down in the front, and is strapped in the back, so you can get into and out of it quickly and easily.

painted backdrop with an American flag on it. This is one time where the photographer definitely does NOT say, "smile" or "cheese." They want you looking all mean and serious – like a Marine should. The photographer says, "Look up here," and before you know it, click click, and you're done, and they're hustling the next recruit into place. It was cool seeing myself in those dress-blues, even if they were "mock."

I bought a gold Marine Corps ring and three yearbooks (which show pictures of 1082 all during training), two composites (little cameos of everyone in 1082), and the biggest picture package you can get – I can't wait to show everyone how I've changed. Wonder what they'll say?

The Donner saga officially ended tonight. He's been sent to MRP (Medical Reconditioning Platoon). Turns out he really did have a legitimate injury. He had what's called shin splints. That's when your shin muscles grow at such a rapid rate that it causes the shinbones to shard. No one in 1082 is sad at all, except Donner himself. Even SDI Bixby is happy. He's been saved the trouble of dropping Donner himself, and having to do a ton of paperwork. I kind of feel bad that I accused him of faking it, but still – plain and simple, he wasn't carrying his weight.

I'm pretty relaxed about the Series Commander Inspection right now, but who knows how I'll feel tomorrow, when he's right in front of me. I'll be getting up about 0300. I'll go into the head, where there's light, to make some final preparations to my uniform. It'll be nice and quiet then – no distractions. I want it to be perfect. Actually, it *must* be perfect!

SATURDAY, MAY 6: TD-35 - ADMINISTRATION WEEK

We did our usual PT and a 3-mile run this morning. PT is pretty tough, but doing it makes me feel *great* afterward. I actually look forward to it. Next, we had the long-awaited Series Commander's Inspection. I was already at the position of attention when he stepped in front of me. "SIR, RECRUIT PRICE, WESTCHESTER, NEW YORK, INFANTRY!"

Next up, you present your weapon to him for inspection, making sure there are no rounds (bullets) in the chamber. My inspection arms rifle movement began well. My rifle passed with flying colors, and before he handed my weapon back, it was time for the knowledge question. The Series Commander asked me to name the famous Marine battle in Korea.

I had heard him ask this question of other recruits, and they had all responded, "NO SIR, THIS RECRUIT DOES NOT KNOW AT THIS TIME, BUT HE WILL FIND THE ANSWER, SIR!"

So when he asked me I said, "SIR, YES SIR. THE BATTLE AT INCHON, SIR!" I sounded off and waited for his response.

"RECRUIT PRICE, DO YOU KNOW YOU ARE THE ONLY RECRUIT TO GET THAT RIGHT IN THE ENTIRE SERIES?"

I could see my Senior give me a look of approval, as my weapon was being handed back to me. Everything was going perfect, I was beaming with pride, so naturally when the Senior gave the command, "PORT ARMS," I fumbled like an idiot to get it done, gave a dumb look of frustration on my face and got hit on for losing my bearing.

Still, it wasn't quite as bad as the recruit to the left of me. The Series Commander, the Marine officer in charge of three platoons, stepped a little too close to him for inspection. Recruit Paventi raised his weapon up to inspect his chamber for a round and cracked the series commander right in the face. It had to hurt, but the lieutenant sucked it up like it never happened. I wouldn't have noticed, had I not been right there.

Everyone is excited about tomorrow's field meet and upcoming BWT (Basic Warrior Training). To get us ready, our DIs took us out back and taught us how to put our hooches (tents) together for the first time today. Recruit Middleton already lost two of his stakes – God knows who has them. The Corps is insane when it comes to details like this. We're screwed if they don't turn up. Whoever wins the meet tomorrow wins the red flag. Tomorrow, 1082 *will* regain the red flag. OOH-RAH!

SUNDAY, MAY 7

We just secured for free time, and it's now 0720. We just made a list of trash we're going to have to bring with us to BWT. Some of these guys are so stupid they can't get anything right – and soon they're gonna be throwing grenades! In church, I said a special prayer that no one gets blown up. Church was pretty good today – and singing the Marines' Hymn was awesome. Soon that will be MY song!

Unfortunately there's no graduation ceremony this week, so we didn't get to see those new Marines to motivate us. After a brief stop in the squad bay to put on some bug juice, we went to the field meet. Capt. Stopa, who is huge and seems to get bigger every time we see him, gave us some words of encouragement, and showed off the trophy for the event. He also let everyone know that their series flag was at stake. This signaled the start of the event. Enthusiasm was high as recruits took part in sprints, mile long runs, hooch preps (tent pitching), pull-ups, sit-ups, push-ups and the tug of war – in which Recruit Price took part. We beat two platoons handily, but then came the final pull for first place.

It was a hard-fought match, and lasted five times longer than the others. My forearms were about to explode I pulled so hard. Unfortunately, we were defeated, and came in 3rd overall. As our reward for third place, we were third in line to eat. We were treated to hot dogs and a cup of juice. I was so hungry, it tasted like champagne and caviar to me. (I'm not really sure what caviar tastes like, but you get the idea). I'm hoping to be stationed in Okinawa after Basic and SOI (School Of Infantry). While we ate, a DI told us that from Okinawa, you can get flights to mainland Japan, Korea, Australia, the Philippines and more for only ten bucks!

We saw Recruit Donner at the meet. Turns out his injury will add another four to five weeks to his training time. I was still a little pissed at him for nearly taking me out with his fall, but I let bygones be bygones. His presence actually motivated us as a platoon. He seemed to be handling his situation well, so he finally earned some respect from 1082. We all have a lot of bruises, including Recruit Price. That's training taking its usual toll, but I still haven't been on sick call once! Knock on wood.

Now we're packing our gear for BWT, and there's nervousness in the air – yet everyone is ready. After all, this is why we all joined the Marines. I have a feeling that this week and next will go extra quickly – and will be extremely important. Especially for Recruit Price, the 0300 Infantry Man. I've decided not to risk bringing this diary with me to

BWT. I'm afraid it might get lost or damaged. Instead, I'll be writing in a tabloid I got at the PX. I'm going to keep it wrapped in a zip-lock baggie. I hope I get time to write. There will also be no outgoing mail, only incoming. I hope I get some.

MONDAY, MAY 8: TD-36

It's 0130, and here I am, making my last head call before BWT, which is just a few hours away. I'm starting to get excited. This week will be physically demanding and mentally challenging, but such things don't scare me anymore. I'm looking forward to facing the challenges, and I know 1082 will be up to it as a platoon. We can be an undisciplined mob at times, but when it comes down to it, we're the best on the Island. Some Third Phase Recruits tried to scare us by telling us that BWT sucks, but we've learned not to listen to that type of trash. If you have the right attitude, nothing sucks.

We just made the "administrative move" to BWT. I still don't know why they don't call it what it is, a freakin' hump. Man, that trash was hard. It was a bitch dragging all our gear to BWT, and some recruits dropped to the deck. One guy from the platoon marching ahead fell and started to do the "funky chicken." The Navy Corpsmen, who are with us for everything we do, quickly came to his care. Turns out he let himself get dehydrated.

The DIs make us drink water for our own good. He probably thought he was getting away with something by not filling his canteen all the way during chug time. As for me, my shoulder was aching like hell, but I kept going anyway. We finally arrived, and set up our hooches (tents). DI Parks was the best – he stayed with us and helped us with pegs and strings to stake out the set-up of our tents. Now, all our hooches are perfectly aligned, while everyone else's are pretty sloppy.

We just ate our first MRE (Meal Ready to Eat). They're pretty nasty – at least breakfast was, anyway. I will never forget it, because it was the only time I've ever eaten "Omelet With Ham." We just had our first class – camouflage. We also got lessons on tactical individual movement, and then actually *did* our individual movements. Next were classes on low crawls, back crawls, incoming rounds and rushing, and scaling walls. For lunch, I had MRE No. 7, and liked it. No. 7 is beef stew, crackers with

Tabasco sauce and a cherry nut cake. After lunch came a class on sanitation, and then dinner, which is served from a hot meal truck. We were all hungry as hell.

After dinner, we all rushed to shower and shave – it was crazy. We almost got into several fistfights over shower space. I used to be a little shy about being naked in front of other guys, but after a couple of months competing with 50 other Recruits for a shower nozzle, you learn you do whatever it takes to get the mission done.

We rushed to get our laundry collected and get mail call in before lights out – but we didn't quite make it. The mail got distributed, but there wasn't enough time to read it. We were ordered to hit the rack, which meant that mail reading would have to wait until tomorrow. I got a letter from Kimball, and I didn't want to wait until tomorrow to read it. I tore it open and stuck it under the crack of my hooch, planning to use the last few minutes of daylight to read it.

The letter had copies of pictures of Kimball's father in WWII, when he was in the Army artillery. He was standing next to his gun, which was marked with one swastika for each Nazi plane he and his men had shot down. Over the pictures, Kirk wrote "FRED KIMBALL, NAZI KILLER!" I laughed, but I was seriously impressed. Then, not even two minutes into reading, I got busted.

SDI Bixby happened to be walking by my hooch and saw me reading. He reached through a crack, grabbed it, and quickly pulled it away. I held my breath waiting for him to pit me on the spot. At this point it was only dusk, but I was so dead tired, I really didn't care what he did to me. I almost felt like yelling, "Hey pal, how about you give me my friggin letter and carry the hell on!" But I guess the picture impressed him, so he just slid it back through the crack and walked away without saying anything. Very decent of him. I barely remembered finishing the letter before I was out cold.

TUESDAY, MAY 9: TD-37

We woke up in the dark this morning, and dressed by the light of our red moonbeams (flashlights). Breakfast was MRE No. 3, chicken stew this time. We did our usual PT and three-mile run. No sweat. I don't think I'd know how to get up without it anymore. Next came a class on

Another picture of Pfc. Price taken while he was in the School of Infantry, following bootcamp. Sometimes the only baths we got to take were in a nearby river or lake.

grenades, then the grenade range – at last! First, we threw two M69 practice grenades. This is to give us the hands-on practice you need to throw the real deal. You get a "DEATH GRIP," and then it's "THUMB CLIP," "PULL PIN," "PREPARE TO THROW GRENADE," and " THROW GRENADE!"

Several recruits made safety violations. They stuck grenade spoons in their helmet covers, to make them look like grenade dunces. This practice also lets the instructors know to be extra wary with them. Then, we threw the M67 fragmentation grenades. They were the same as the practice grenades, baseball-size, but that's where the difference ends. It was by *far* the biggest firecracker I've ever thrown, and what an awesome feeling it was throwing it. I felt like the Mighty Thor, throwing lightning bolts!

Several recruits have been getting some minor injuries which are actually just ongoing aches and pains. They've been trying to ignore them, but you can tell they're in serious pain, and only getting worse. Recruits Collins, Hockenberry and Phillips are questionable for Thursday's Combat Conditioning Course. I'm worried about Collins – he's a good-to-go kid, and he seems to have hurt his leg pretty bad.

Next came more bayonet training, lunch, yet another MRE, and a fire team leadership class. For dinner, we ate another quick chow from the hot meal truck, then came another quick as hell shower and shave with 50 naked and nasty recruits fighting for shower and mirror space.

We also took a night individual-movement class today, and now we're actually doing it. There were all kinds of trails, covered with booby traps. One false move and BLAMMO, you're "dead!" Everyone from the series was split up and waiting on different trails to enter the trip flare course. Slowly and quietly, you check for trip wires using the methods they taught us, and you maneuver successfully to the end of the trail.

When a flare is launched, everyone hits the deck so as not to silhouette himself and give his position away. Then, a mine went off. In the darkness you could hear a recruit from Platoon 1080 sound off, "Recruit Rogers from Platoon 1080 is dead!" then another one, then a third one. Their DI screamed, "HOW COME EVERYONE FROM MY FREAKIN PLATOON IS DYING?!?!?" It was pretty funny the way he said it. We only lost one man from 1082 – a small success.

Before I forget, there was one other story that cracked me up.
Picture how dark it was that night. There was only about 30 percent
illumination from the moon, and we were in the middle of the woods.
Everyone was wearing cammies, including the DIs. So our DI goes up
to Recruit Hill and tells him to look at the recruit 20 yards away, just
standing there.

"YOU SEE THAT STINKIN' RECRUIT THERE?"

"YES, SIR."

"WELL, NEXT TIME A FLARE GOES OFF, YOU TEACH HIM TO
HIT THE DECK!"

"YES, SIR." Sure enough, at the next flare, Hillman took off and
just rammed the guy into the dirt. That's when all hell broke loose.
Turns out it wasn't a recruit at all – it was a DI! And not just any DI,
but the one who told me I was lazy and called me a little girl. Ahh,
sweet revenge! He freaked out, but Hillman knew better than to stick
around and escaped into the darkness. Of course, our DI knew exactly
what he was doing. He had planned the whole thing perfectly.

Something weird happened to Recruit Clayton tonight. I think he
sort of flipped out. He just started walking away from the bivouac
(camp) site. SDI Bixby ran after him screaming, but he didn't respond.
When Bixby finally led him back to bivouac, he was really despondent.
I sort of know how he felt. It does make you a little crazy, the way they
take away everything you used to be and replace it with a new Marine
attitude. You just have to learn to like it. Not everyone can – but
Recruit Price sure as hell can. I never thought I'd get used to Marine
life, but I have. They've made me into a new man, and I'm damn proud
of the changes they've made in me.

As it turned out, Clayton got a "Dear John" letter from his fiancée.
It never ceases to amaze me how girlfriends think they have the worst
of it, lasting three months alone. Meanwhile, in the same three months,
we are each going through our own personal hells. All I can say is, it is
her loss, and I hope Clayton can get through it all right.

We racked out at 2300. I used to party until dawn, but this was the
latest I'd been up in months.

WEDNESDAY, MAY 10: TD-38

Today they let us sleep late – all the way to 0630. After chow, we hit a tactical formation class, then we formed into fire teams and set off for the courses. Our team crept through five or six different areas using the hand signals we'd learned so far. For the first time this week (not counting tossing that awesome frag grenade), I'm enjoying myself. It feels great to be part of a team, working together and relying on one another.

From there, we just sat on our gear and exercised the ever-popular Marine adage, "Hurry up and wait," for the rest of the series to finish. It was then that I met a Corporal Snyder of the Public Affairs Division. He told me a friend of mine who works in the media called, asking if it was possible to get photographs of me training, for a magazine article. Kimball strikes again!

"What makes *you* so special?" Snyder asked me.

"NOTHING, SIR," I told him. But I do feel special to have a friend like that. (And now you know how I got some of the pictures that appear in this book, including the cover shot!)

Then we were back on the "hardball" a.k.a. "street," stepping it out. We weren't really sure where we were going, but we all had an idea. That's when we saw it. The Marine Corps Rappelling Tower. The first order of business was to get a class on what's called your "Swiss Seat." The Swiss Seat is the rope that is tied around your waist and bottom for support that ties into the main rappel line. It's a pretty wicked series of knots up and under, down and through here and so forth. Needless to say, I screwed mine up.

As hard as I was trying to get it perfect, I was pretty nervous. I thought the instructor, this really big and mean Spanish guy, was going to chew my ass. Instead he came over and quickly fixed it for me. When I tell you he made it tight, I thought my ass was going to explode! In this type of exercise, there is no room for error. I felt assured my Swiss Seat was good to go. The tighter the better.

While we were busy getting all bound up, our DIs were already on top of the tower. They were ready to give us our next period of instruction and it was quite impressive. They showed us the different ways to come down, which included how we should do it, and more importantly, how we should *not* do it. They went down regular, running forward, bounding, all the time using their weak hand to squeeze the rope that's held behind the back, used for slowing and stopping whenever necessary.

Then came our DI, Wight. He was like a madman. He ran off the tower screaming and rappelled over two-thirds of the way in one bound, before he was stopped on the dime by the DI holding the safety line. At first we didn't realize he had it planned like that. We thought the crazy bastard was doing his best Wily Coyote impression.

So you see, there's absolutely nothing to be scared of. Right? Wrong. When I had finally climbed the five stories and looked down, my stomach was not happy. Not at all. I could feel that old MRE starting to report for duty. I could see some recruits keep letting others skip ahead of them, trying to put off the inevitable. That only made it easier to step up to the plate for me. There are several ditties like "THE GATE IS OPEN," and "THE GATE IS CLOSED," to signify that you are tied in. Then comes the good stuff. "RECRUIT PRICE ON RAPPEL!"

And from down below, "STAFF SERGEANT JONES ON RELAY!" (Meaning that he had the safety rope and was ready to go). Then the Instructor counts "1... 2... 3..." and lets me go until I was perpendicular to the rappel wall. Then I released with my weak hand, and began my descent. When I realized how in control I was, it was one of the greatest things I had ever done. It was extremely intense. Carolyn Price's little boy was actually scaling down a wall, 47 feet off the ground!

Next, I did the simulated helo (helicopter) drop. This one is a little different, because there is no bulkhead. You just drop through the air. I have to admit it was pretty scary being on top of that 47-foot high tower, but after it was all said and done, I loved it. Watching and then doing it kept reminding me of the old Batman TV show, when Batman and Robin used to scale walls with their Bat-ropes, only now it was platoon 1082 doing it, and the camera was not rotated to make it look real – it *was* real!

SDI Bixby is doing his best to give our injured recruits, Collins and Hockenberry, a rest. They're both dead tired, so he assigned them to hooch guard. Got to hand it to Bixby – he really looks out for us, and tries to go easy on us when we deserve it. But truthfully, we don't deserve it much.

Tonight, Recruits Pomrink and Price pulled fire watch. Even in the middle of the night, a lot of recruits were talking in their hooches. It was my responsibility to quiet them down. I didn't particularly enjoy that, but I've learned to do a lot of things I didn't used to enjoy without complaint. I tried to quiet them down without being demeaning.

I could hear the DIs talking by the fireside during my fire watch duty. They were telling some pretty funny stories about watching punk rockers go through receiving when they arrived on the Island. Man were they shocked by those haircuts! Their original hair styles sure did buy them a lot of extra attention.

Speaking of hair styles reminds me that I was so busy today, I didn't have time to miss my usual Wednesday cut – too busy learning how to become a warrior. I can't believe it was only a couple of months ago that I arrived here. So much has happened since then it seems like years.

Our new DI, Ojeda, showed me my first BWT raccoon. Parris Island lore has it that there are raccoons the size of grizzlies out there in the BWT training area. This one was pretty small, but his size didn't stop him from busting into Ojeda's hooch to look for an early morning snack. Time passed, and slowly it turned from dark to light. Almost time for another intense day of Marine training.

THURSDAY, MAY 11: TD-39

Today we did the Combat Conditioning Course or CCC – one of the requirements for graduation. We had to do the rope climb wearing uniforms, deuce gear (war gear), helmet and rifle. Only one nasty recruit from 1082 failed – Shales again. He had no problem doing it before, when it didn't count. He just lets the pressure eat him up. After he failed it the first time, he made it on the second attempt, when by all rights, he should have been weaker. It was because everyone had already left and wasn't watching, so he didn't feel so pressured.

Next came our usual morning three-mile run, but this time wearing full gear, like we did climbing up the rope, except minus the Kevlar helmet. It was hard, but not too hard. All of 1082 made it, but at least three others from different platoons did not. They get one more chance tomorrow, and if they fail then it's off to the dreaded PCP (Physical Conditioning Platoon).

Next came the fireman's carry. I had 45 seconds to run 100 meters with 6' 7," 220-pound recruit Snedeker on my back and shoulders. A few recruits dropped their man, and had to do it again. I screamed the whole way, which got the adrenaline flowing, making it seem easier. After that, we rushed down to the field, getting in our high and low crawls. Everyone passed the CCC except our two recruits who are injured and still on hooch duty. Their fate is unknown.

We raced back to camp and broke down our hooches, then moved to the sea huts. These are buildings with screen windows all the way round and are full of bunk beds. There are no mattresses, but compared to the hooches and getting rained on, it was like staying at the Holiday Inn. From there, we left to march to another class.

During the march, my bunkmate Recruit Pomrink started asking me some questions. We're not supposed to talk while marching, but I was in a daze and I didn't even think to not answer him. You guessed it – I got busted. I was immediately pitted, and while I was being punished, I missed some orders. We were told to take our rifles, but I thought we were supposed to leave them. After cranking out about 100 pushups, my Senior saw me and told me to get up, and get in formation. As I returned through the back door, everyone was leaving through the front. I got the idea as I walked outside and saw everyone with their weapons. I turned to grab my rifle, but DI Wight was about to get it for me. He grabbed it at the same time I did.

"LET GO! LET IT GO!" Wight screamed at me. I felt like we were in the middle of a Leggo Waffle commercial.

"I am nothing without my rifle," I thought. They've got us trained to value our rifles over just about everything, and I felt like fighting him for it. I held firmly, not budging an inch.

"LET IT GO PRICE, LET IT GO!!" He continued.

Finally, I saw that he wasn't playing around any more. For better or worse, I released it and fell out as ordered. Eventually, he did give it back to me, by throwing it on the deck. I was so friggin' mad I thought I was going to bust, but I did NOT lose my bearing. Recruit Price learned that lesson a long time ago, and will not forget it.

We had classes on helicopter landings and amphibious landings. Most of the BWT classes are outdoors, but some are inside. Today, we sat inside what looked like an old warehouse building. We had been here before, for the camouflage class. There are about six rows of tables with really long benches to sit on. The building is pretty stuffy, even with fans going, making a not-so-great atmosphere for taking instruction. It's also not too brightly lit. So, despite the motivation that spills out of every Parris Island instructor and the pumped-up high we had from rappelling, we were all starting to drag. I looked around and could see some recruits' heads nodding up and down, trying to fight the sleep off. I even saw DI Ojeda fighting the sandman!

After the class, they knew we were tired, so they got us all pumped up with some pushups and mountain climbers. Then, we were double-timed over to another training area. There were some mock helo's and an Amtrak. They were made out of plywood, but you get the idea. For the next two hours, we did practical application or 'prac-ap,' to make sure we didn't forget what we were just taught. I'm beginning to dig this commando trash. I really flew out of the mock helo. I was one of the two last guys, so we provided security and made sure everyone was off the helo, and then we joined the rest of our squad in the tree line.

When we got back to our bivouac, we were looking all nasty. We had cammie paint all over the place, pinecones and needles stuck in our uniforms. We were sweaty, tired and scraped up from diving in the brush. Then we see Recruits Collins and Hockenberry, all clean after their watch. The word on them is they have been given ten days to get better, and then they *must* complete the CCC.

After dinner and another shower-and-shave riot, we came back to the sea hut. Platoon 1082 rushed like hell to get the place and all our gear squared away. Recruit Clayton was on sick call after his mysterious episode a few days ago, Recruit Shales was also on sick call, and Donner has gone to MRP – so tonight, for a brief moment, Recruit Price was squad leader. It felt pretty good to be in front of 1082, leading the way. I know I'm not a real Marine yet, but I'm now feeling more like a Marine than a civilian, and I'm liking that feeling a whole lot.

DI Parks gave us on our first free time in quite a while. He even let us go outside! I chose to stay inside, so I could write my journal while it was still light out. I couldn't resist going outside for long, though. I went out, sat by a tree, read some letters I had gotten, and just relaxed. Having a whole hour to myself allowed my mind to wander... what would it be like to actually have an entire *day* or *weekend*? Ahh to dream, but I won't be dreaming for long. No sir!

FRIDAY, MAY 12: TD-40

Woke up at 0500. During BWT, we sleep on mattress springs and isomats – making for a rough night. To make matters worse, I'm coming down with something. I felt really dizzy for a minute today. I told SDI Bixby, and I'm waiting to go on sick call. Only three more weeks to go until graduation, and now I have to get sick. DI Wight says, "PAIN IS TEMPORARY! PAIN IS JUST WEAKNESS LEAVING THE BODY!" I feel like a lot of "weakness" is leaving mine right now.

The march to mapping class was only two miles, but it felt like it took forever. I must be sick. My biggest worry is the Gas Chamber tomorrow. We have to go into a small room wearing gasmasks, then remove them and say our names, ranks and social security numbers out loud. This forces us to get a nice lung-full of gas. It's one of the nine major requirements for graduation, and I can't allow whatever's wrong with me to make me fail it. Not to mention, I don't want the Senior to think that I am faking it because I'm scared to be gassed. I mean, I *am* nervous as hell, but I'd feel like a total shitbird if my DIs thought I was lying. I'm just going to stick it out, no matter *what*.

As I write this, I'm in my sixth hour of mapping class. Everything's a competition here – they even made a contest out of finding coordinates on a map. In a close race, 1082 pulled out a win. We're all dead tired – I saw both of our DIs, Ojeda and Parks, fighting the sleep bug, and not faring too well either.

I can definitely feel the attitude of a Third Phase Recruit coming on. I almost pulled a nasty recruit off the hot truck during dinner tonight. They never serve us enough, and after one gave me a particularly meager amount of chow, I gave him a dirty look. Remember too, that this little turd is on his Mess & Maintenance Week. I know exactly how much food he is stuffing his fat face with, because I was just there myself, stuffing *my* fat face. When he opened his mouth to me, I lost it.

"Well, at least it's hot," he told me. As opposed to MREs, which are cold unless you use the heater that is included, only we never have the time.

"At least it's hot?" I replied, "Shut your friggin mouth! How about we go step over to the tree line and I teach you some manners?" I could see he was starting to look a little nervous, because he refused to make eye contact.

Then Recruit Lugo, doing his best DI-voice imitation, says, "Listen here, you stinkin' nasty recruit, how would you like it if I stick that ladle right up your freakin' ass?" Fearing the attention of our DIs, we both backed off and gave the guy some neighborly advice: "We'll see how you like it when *you* get to Third Phase, and *your* ass only gets this one meal a day!"

Actually, we were just messing with him. We're still getting our "Three Hots and a Cot." Two of those meals are MREs, but they are still meals. I could just picture this guy telling his whole platoon how you only get one meal a day during BWT.

Hope I get some more motivating letters tonight. After dealing with that little jerk-off, I can use the encouragement.

SATURDAY, MAY 13: TD-41

Twenty days and a wake-up to graduation. First, however, Platoon 1082 had to survive today's mind-numbing Gas Chamber attack. The first order of business was to give us instruction on how to don and clear an M40 gas mask, which means we learned how to put on a mask and clear it of any toxins before we start to breath into it. Next, we were given our MOPP suits. That stands for Mission Oriented Protective Posture. We got to wear the tops and bottoms. It wouldn't be long now.

Everyone was a little afraid, and with good cause. The day we got our pictures taken in mock dress-blues, the civilians in charge of sales showed us a video of Parris Island Recruits. What made the biggest impression on us were scenes of recruits exiting the Gas Chamber, with snot and puke all over their faces. They were NOT happy campers. I was feeling better from that flu thing, and confident I'd do okay, or so I convinced myself. In the class before gas attack, everybody was moving around and talking more than they should have. They were way too loose, until they got to the part where we learned to check for malfunctions in the gas mask. Suddenly, everyone was all ears and asking this question and that. We were all afraid our masks would have a leak. Then the countdown began.

Everyone was put in separate lines. Forty recruits at a time were to enter the "Chamber." Above the entrance to the gas chamber was a big sign, "EVEN THE BRAVE CRY HERE." Suddenly we were all on edge. The first group entered and no sooner had they gotten in, then one recruit came flying back out. He caught a whiff of something he didn't like, and exploded through the door before the DIs could even respond.

At this point, we were all like, "What the hell goes on in there??" As the lines moved up, I was right by a window, so I started sneaking a look. Big mistake on my part. There were already fumes seeping out of the building. My eyes got a little taste of burning. One recruit put his mask on early – and got it yanked right off.

"YOU DON'T PUT ON YOUR DOGGONE MASK UNTIL I TELL YOU TO, RECRUIT!"

Then, as if on cue, the DI boomed, "NEXT WAVE! DON YOUR MASKS AND ENTER THE CHAMBER!!"

We put on our masks, and entered the chamber one recruit at a time. In a few seconds – POP, POP, POP – gas pellets were dropped in the chamber. We made a big rectangle up against the walls. In the middle of the room, we could see the gray smoke of the gas starting to combine with the gas from previous waves.

We all started to give the signal for contact with gas, "GAS, GAS, GAS!!" with the appropriate hand and arm signal. When Recruit Medina gave his signal, he started to lose it! He didn't have his mask on properly with an airtight seal. In seconds, gas was all over him. He instinctively bolted and ran for the door. SDI Bixby grabbed him and tried to get his mask on right.

"PUT THAT MASK ON, MEDINA!" Bixby shouted.

"No," Medina started screaming, "No, I can't, there is no air!"

"PUT THAT FRIGGIN' MASK ON!" Bixby screamed.

Medina started thrashing around like a wild man. He was kicking and screaming, basically doing everything he wasn't supposed to do. So DI Parks ran over and helped drag Medina outside to get him some air. When he calmed down about 15 minutes later, they sent him right back in. There is no easy escape from your stay in the gas chamber. You either do it successfully and continue to the next stage of training, or you freak out and have to go through it all over again.

Back in the gas chamber, we next had to remove our masks and say our name, rank and Social Security numbers out loud. This forces even the best to gulp in a good amount of gas. Recruit Stitchberry tried to get away without saying it, and made a bolt for the door, also.

A few DIs, who were only too happy to do it, rammed him up against the wall. One psychopath recruit seemed to be enjoying it. He was actually yelling out his information and going "YEAH, YEAH, GET SOME, GET SOME!" Go figure. Anyway, next it was my turn.

"RECRUIT PRICE," I shouted, "PRIVATE FIRST CLASS, 107-86-5643." After I had said it, the instructor could obviously see I had broken my seal. He waited, but not as long as I had expected. I donned and cleared my mask, and was surprised to see I was still alive. I opened my eyes and there was only a minor bit of burning.

When everyone was done, we faced left, grabbing the man ahead of us, and started to file out. How could this be the rough and tough ordeal everyone was so afraid of? Well, I shouldn't have asked. The DIs had one final ace up their sleeves. Just as we were leaving the entrance, they were yelling at us to, "TAKE YOUR GAS MASK OFF, TAKE YOUR STINKIN' MASKS OFF!" I thought no problem. I could see daylight, what's the worst that could happen? I soon found out.

Even though I was physically outside of the building, there were still a good deal of fumes still in the air and following us outside the chamber. The DIs continued to bark out orders, "WALK WITH YOUR ARMS OUT, OPEN YOUR EYES, OPEN YOUR NASTY EYEBALLS RECRUITS!" As soon as I complied, I was done for. Wow, does that

Look out! Here comes Recruit Price gagging and spitting after leaving the Gas Chamber. This exercise gets you familiar with CS-Riot Control gas, and teaches you how to properly don and clear a gas mask.

tear gas – a.k.a. CS Riot Control gas – clear out your sinuses. It also just about blinds you. As I stumbled out of the chamber, I was covered with snot and drool – my eyes were so full of tears I couldn't see.

Every time I tried to open my eyes to comply with the DIs, the snot and tears got worse. It was then, out of the corner of my eye, I could see a video camera was filming the whole thing. Even though I was in a great deal of misery, I was laughing at myself, picturing how funny I must have looked. On top of the snot, I was spitting up a lung.

After the second time, a DI screamed, "THE NEXT NASTY RECRUIT WHO SPITS ON MY DECK IS GOING RIGHT BACK IN FOR SOME MORE!"

I heard his words perfectly, but my body overrode the command. Not even two seconds later, I spat another gas chamber loogie on the deck. "WHO DID IT? WHO'S THE SLIMY BASTARD WHO SPIT ON MY DECK?"

As much as I dreaded going through this wonderful experience again, I owned up. I really thought I would have to return to the chamber, but once again SDI to the rescue. He gathered up all his lost sheep, who had already finished, into one area.

We were told to take off our MOPP suits and throw them in a pile, then we sat in formation waiting for the rest of the platoon to finish. We had a bird's eye view of the recruits exiting the chamber. Some recruit from another platoon started to wander away from the chain because he still had his eyes closed. He didn't really hurt himself, but we enjoyed watching as he walked right into a telephone pole! Only our screaming at him to stop saved him from really ramming into it.

We watched as some of the more caring DIs allowed their recruits to rub their eyes to soothe the pain. Only what was on their hands when they rubbed? You guessed it, more gas. What a bitch that gas chamber was – but less than 10 minutes later it wore off, and we were back to the familiar business of cleaning our rifles.

Our next and last class was Nuclear Biological Chemical warfare. Recruits are falling asleep everywhere, including the two on both sides of me as I write this. I have to keep waking them up. The way we wake up our fellow recruits is pretty funny. We give them a slap on the back of the neck! How hard depends on if you really like the guy or not.

Sometimes, when it is a friend, you slap him harder just for fun. Today, I felt like I was playing recruit bongos.

Recruit Hockenberry even fell asleep after he had volunteered to hold the clicker for the slides. The instructor was telling him to advance to the next slide, and there was Hockenberry, out cold! It was a riot, but not for him. He was taken outside and didn't return until he was nice and sweaty.

After another motivating MRE, we prepared our gear for a long afternoon of training. With SDI Bixby in the lead, we hit the NBC trail to practice what the few Recruits who stayed awake – including Recruit Price – learned. First, we incorporated what we had learned from the patrolling classes as we formed a platoon long 'tactical column' formation. We proceeded down the trail, keeping an eye out for anything unusual. When DI Gaita popped out of nowhere, he screamed, "CHEMICAL AIR ATTACK!"

We donned gas masks (again) and covered our weapons and ourselves completely with our ponchos. During instruction, we were told that in a chemical air attack you have approximately nine seconds to get completely covered. Our new DI, Ojeda, was screaming because a lot of us were slow. Many of us took over twenty seconds!

Sgt. Gaita, the other platoon's DI, who hates us because we constantly make his platoon look like shit, saw his chance to let us have it. "HURRY IT UP! THIRTY OF YOU NASTY RECRUITS WOULD HAVE BEEN DEAD ALREADY! I'D BE BETTER OFF SHOOTING MYSELF IN THE FOOT THAN SERVING WITH A BUNCH OF NASTY THINGS LIKE YOU! THE ONLY THING YOU GUYS KNOW HOW TO DO QUICKLY IS EAT YOUR FOOD, AND WRITE LETTERS TO YOUR FAT GIRLFRIENDS!"

He was correct. If this had been a real combat situation, it *would* have been lethal for many. Unlike other branches, the Marines *NEVER* leave behind their dead or wounded, and no platoon could survive with 20 men carrying 30 fallen.

Afterward, we received a twenty-minute ass chewing session on how slow we were, and we practiced the procedure another 20 times, until we could do it. The Marine Corps is big on stressing the muscle memory concept. The idea behind it is that if you do something many times in a row, your brain processes meld with your muscle movements. Before you know it, you don't even have to think, your body's muscles just naturally react. Officially, for this to work, it takes closer to 2,000 run-throughs, not 20. But who's counting?

We regrouped and hit the trail once more. Along the way we were confronted by another DI.

"CHEMICAL AGENTS HAVE ALREADY BEEN RELEASED AND YOU'RE UNDER ATTACK!" After we having just been reamed, Platoon 1082 knew exactly what to do. We all started screaming "GAS, GAS, GAS!" followed by "INCOMING!" We got masked and hit the deck, with our weapons underneath us. Our helmets were all facing the blast area for protection, and our hands were underneath our bodies.

"NOT BAD, NOT BAD! YOU MAGGOTS MUST BE PAYING ATTENTION IN YOUR CLASSES!" I laughed to myself. If he had been there 30 minutes ago, he would have had a very different opinion.

At this point, we were all wondering if we were going to see any more gas – real gas that is. We had heard rumors that somewhere along the trail we would get gassed, but the day was almost at its end. No sooner had I thought this, than we entered a decent sized clearing and out of nowhere, a huge Navy Corpsman comes charging at us with a huge gas canister stuck on the end of a broomstick-sized pole! We sort of knew he was coming, but it was *still* a surprise. I barely got my mask on in time. I could see the fumes starting to blow quickly toward me, but I only suffered some minor eye irritation. My head was racing, but I kept my bearing and donned and cleared like a pro.

Once again, poor old Recruit Medina wasn't so lucky. He started fumbling for his mask, but it was useless. The fumes all ready had him, so he reverted back to his instincts and tried to make a run for it. Wrong move. The DIs grabbed him, shouting for him to put on his mask. He kept thrashing around like a madman screaming, "I CAN'T, I CAN'T!" They were trying to hold him down to help him, but all he knew was that people were all over him. He had taken in some gas already, so it was no great wonder when he started throwing DIs off.

SDI Bixby was the first to get thrown. Then our Series Gunnery Sergeant, who is huge, got knocked back. Finally, DI Parks came flying in for the kill. He wrapped Medina up and tossed him down to stay. As Medina's reward for being so difficult, they held a canister right under his nose to make their point.

Other recruits also had some problems. With all the attention on Medina, no one stopped Recruit Pechette from taking off. While dodging the gas, he rammed into Recruit Hillman so hard, he almost knocked him out cold. Later on, during free time, Pechette denied he ran. He denied it to avoid us ragging on him, something we like to do daily. Normally, this was his typical annoying behavior, but I could see Recruit Hillman fuming. I saw him do it, Hillman saw him do it, and Hill's ribs were still sore from it. Every time Pechette denied it, I could see Hill's eyes getting redder and redder. When I talked to Hillman later, he told me, "I'm going to get that son of a bitch reservist! You watch, Price, old fat-boy Pechette is going to get his!"

The day's exercises finished with a class on how to decontaminate yourself and change over into another MOPP suit when yours has already received chemical agents, and a class on how to drink water with your gas mask on. There is a straw tube that sticks into your canteen cap. Eating is another story. We will not ever be in a situation where full MOPP gear is worn 24-7, hopefully, but we could go a day or two without grub. As for using the head, that is a question you can save for your DI. I don't think you really *want* to know the answer. Suffice it to say that if you think you are in danger of entering a chemical-danger area, it would be best to go to the bathroom *before* getting suited up!

We ended the day with one more bomb blasting nearby. "INCOMING!" We all hit the deck with our hands in crouch position, belly down, covering our precious rifle. "I am nothing without my rifle!"

We had learned many things today, how to check for radiation, decontaminate ourselves and gear, drink water with gas masks on, MOPP suit levels, how to clean our eyes of chemicals and much more. We marched back to the gas chamber area, tired and bruised, but not beaten. All our gear was right where we left it, and there were buses already waiting for us. We arrived back just in time too, because out on the horizon there was a wicked lightning and thunderstorm on the way. I hoped it wasn't a sign of bad things to come.

Then we jammed on a bus for A-Line. As we rode on the bus, we passed by lots of groups of recruits, all in different stages of training. Parris Island is just like a factory assembly line, devoted to fine-tuning recruits and pumping out the best "products" it can. Civilians jump off the bus, hit the yellow footprints, then they're moved along the line quickly. Their nasty civilian hair, clothes and attitudes are taken away. As they move along the line, they're instilled with discipline, pride and respect. Some products get messed up at one stage or another, so they're sent back to the assembly line.

Other products get completely messed up, and they get stamped REJECTED. All they have to remember the factory by is $25, a bus ticket home, and a bald head. Platoon1082 has moved along from the start of the assembly line to near the end. We lost some products along the way, gained some new ones, and now we're almost ready to be put on the market – brand new men, brand new Marines.

When we arrived at our new home for A-Line, a series of buildings called "The White Elephants," we stowed all our gear, then fell out into the back as ordered. Once there, we spent the rest of the day remediating some BWT knowledge for the final test coming up this Friday. We broke up into study groups and quizzed ourselves on all we had learned. We were never so happy to see the hot truck chugging around the side of our building. Chow had arrived. The recruits on the hot truck actually gave us an ample serving for the first time. Maybe our little talk the other day paid off.

Later DI Wight put us in the rack and told us a ghost story about the White Elephants we were living in. "It all started around 30 years ago. The recruits from this very building were given the order to field-day (clean) the barracks. When their DI returned to inspect, he found them out in the back 'smoking and joking.' He was livid. He ordered them out front, in formation, in full gear and proceeded to take them on a death march. When they started to hump through an area called Ribbon Creek, he did not take the tide into consideration. He'd never been there at this time of the night, so he never saw coming what happened next.

When the water level jumped from knee level to chest, his men – in full gear – were in big trouble. As the water level increased, the DI ordered everyone back, but it was too late. He desperately started to pull recruits out, but by then it was too late. He lost over half his platoon that night, and if you listen real closely, you can still hear those recruits crying out for help.

As I looked around, I could see some recruits eating up his every word. I had remembered my uncle telling me this story. I know that what happened at Ribbon Creek was a true story, but the ghost part I cannot confirm. The DI went on. "And this area is where they come at night. You watch, late at night, you'll hear things, noises you can't explain. Everyone does. You'll see. Good night ladies. Rest easy!"

After he was gone, the guys couldn't stop talking about it. I wasn't quite ready to rack out just yet. So, I busted out the pen and paper I was hiding underneath my pillow. I thought he was gone, but no sooner had I written "Dear Mom," than he caught me. Writing an after-lights-out letter by the light of a moonbeam (flashlight) is a big no-no. He confiscated both letter and moonbeam. Good thing it wasn't this diary. Nineteen days and a wake-up to graduation! OOH-RAH!

SUNDAY, MAY 14 *(Mother's Day)*

Time on deck: 0515. Platoon 1082 is waking up for the first breakfast we've seen in chow hall in a loooong time. Recruit Price broke out of his normal diet of yogurt, fruit, and cereal today, and added French toast, a bear claw, and eggs. It tasted good, good, good! After chow, the Senior opened the floor to talk about the joys of being gassed. After having our little pow-wow about the gas chamber, I had to laugh at how funny it is that we were already joking about the thing we had dreaded only a day ago. Even Medina, who went through the worst of it, managed a few smiles.

Now we're on free time. While we were still somewhat on the subject, I asked Hillman privately if he was still mad at Pechette for slamming into him and then denying it later. He told me he wasn't mad at all, at least not after last night. Apparently, while everyone was sleeping, our PT gear was being washed and dried by the recruits on fire watch.

During *his* watch, Hillman snuck over and put some "Icy Hot" in Pechette's jock strap. He told some others and myself, so for once we were all dying to go PT to see how Pechette was going to react. To keep busy, I got caught up on letters home. I wrote letters to Mom, John, and Kimball. I couldn't think of anybody else I wanted to write, so here I am

Even during the training and the firing of weapons at A-Line, somehow SDI Bixby always found plenty of time to take us on PT (Physical Training) runs.

making my daily "Devil Dog Diary" entry.

During our 1/4-mile drill march coming back from lunch chow, I thought we were doing fine, but DI Parks was in a bad mood. The sand fleas were biting like crazy. They were all over us – and no one had on any bug juice. Apparently some of the recruits marching behind us were pretty sloppy. They weren't driving their heels, I think.

One recruit had lost his soft cover, so he looked stupid enough marching to and from chow with his helmet on, but to make it worse, he accidentally had it on backward. He looked like an ass, with his name tape facing forward. Top this with DI Wight catching a lot of us scratching, including – you guessed it – me, and we had the makings for a serious thrashing.

He got right in my face as always, "YOU DISGUST ME PRICE. WHEN I CALL FOR YOU LATER, YOU HAD BETTER BE THERE. YOU WILL KNOW WHEN."

"Great," I thought, there goes our Sunday.

SDI Bixby was upset by our performance too. In fact, I cannot remember him ever being so upset, not since he watched Recruit Donner's pathetic attempts to climb up the rope. He began to let us have it.

"WHAT IN THE HELL IS WRONG WITH YOU GUYS TODAY? YOU GUYS DON'T WANT TO MARCH? THAT'S FINE, YOU WANT TO MARCH LIKE SHIT, YOU WANT TO MAKE ME LOOK STUPID, WELL THEN LET ME HELP YOU GUYS OUT!" He began calling all kinds of drill movements at once. "TO THE REAR... MARCH," "LEFT OBLIQUE...MARCH," FORWARD MARCH, TO THE REAR, MARCH."

All of this was coming fast and furious, all on the wrong foot. It wasn't long before we were a marching disaster. I hated it. As much as I dislike drill, making us march like that was really burning me up. After what seemed like an eternity of us marching like fools, we found ourselves falling out and flying into our squad bay.

After a nasty field day, the Senior wanted to take us for one of his PT sessions. Normally his Sunday PT is to help us keep in shape and work on our weaknesses, mainly things like the rope and pull-ups. Well, today, we did it all. Push-ups, pull-ups, sit ups, the 'O' Course, lunges, to name a few. In one category, I was real happy. We did max sets of sit ups in two minutes, then a max set in 1 1/2 minutes, then 1 minute, then 30 seconds. In two minutes, Recruit Price finally did 80 sit-ups today. I did come close to busting my gut, but I did it! OOH-RAH! By the time we got in formation to run back to the barracks, I had forgotten all about Recruit Pechette's icy-hot, burning jock. I glanced over at him and almost broke out laughing when I saw the expression on his face. He looked like he was going to explode, and he couldn't stop from fidgeting.

"PECHETTE, WHAT IN THE F IS YOUR STORY *TODAY*, PROBLEM CHILD?" the senior roared.

"SIR, THIS RECRUIT DON'T KNOW."

"WELL THEN EXPLAIN TO ME WHY YOU ARE MOVING IN MY FORMATION, AND IT HAD BETTER BE GOOD!"

"SIR, THIS RECRUIT FEELS LIKE HIS BALLS ARE ABOUT TO EXPLODE!!" At this point, I could see the senior wanted to laugh, but he held back. He ordered Pechette, "FALL OUT, CRAB BOY!" In honor of his new name, the senior had him crab-crawl all the way back to the barracks. We were already coming out of the showers when Crab Boy made his return. Senior told him to completely field day the entire head by himself, and to not come out of the shower until he no longer had his mystery itch. Later on, I could tell Hillman was quite pleased with his revenge.

After PT, SDI Bixby was still disgusted with us. He decided it was time to furl up the red flag, a big slap in the face otherwise known as the "Tampon on a stick." He wanted to give 1082 a wake-up call, so we wouldn't think we're already on the bus headed home for liberty and our sweet Suzies (girlfriends). To continue driving the message home and show us he wasn't fooling around this time, he marched us to lunch chow telling us he was going to get nasty, as nasty could be.

We marched by another platoon, looking like shit due to all the commands we were being assaulted with. If we hadn't felt stupid earlier, we sure did now. To make matters worse, after chow, DI Wight cashed in his chips from earlier. I was hoping he would have forgotten by now.

"ALL RIGHT, LET'S GO LADIES, IF YOU OWE ME, YOU KNOW WHO YOU ARE! DON'T MAKE ME GET YOU!"

Between the scratching in the morning and getting caught writing that letter last night, I knew there was no escaping this one.

"OH, AND DON'T FORGET YOUR RIFLES! YOU'LL BE NEEDING THEM."

There were no sandpits behind the White Elephants, so we made up for it with rifle PT. Altogether, he had seven of us out there. He started us off with push-ups, then he made us hold our rifle extended straightforward while running in place for what seemed like forever. It was the hardest (non-pit) pit call yet. When we started to do squats with the rifle held straight out, I thought I was going to drop, but managed to hold up. As we stopped half way down and held there, Recruit Butler started to moan and grunt like a little bitch.

At first he was angering me, but then DI Wight started making fun of him. "BUTLER, WHAT'S THE MATTER, BUTLER? WE DON'T LIKE THIS? ARE WE GETTING MAD?" Soon, instead of annoying me, Butler's moaning only motivated me. I tuned into his whining and found that it took my mind off of the pain. "Suck it up, Butler!" I yelled at him, "You should hear yourself!"

The sun was starting to set, but it was still a hot day. We were only five or six minutes into our little "session," and already drenched in sweat. With the veins in my arms about ready to pop and sweat running down into my eyes (with no way to wipe it away), I was no happy camper.

By now, I believe Wight knew who was putting out and started letting us go one by one. "DAVIS, GO! BATES, GO! PRICE, GO!" As he let us leave, I noticed he had rewarded the recruits who didn't bitch and moan by letting us go. As you might have guessed, Recruit Butler was last to leave.

It was great to eat real chow today for dinner. I probably ate too much, but after that trip to the pit, I felt I deserved it. Before rack-out, we set up our H-harnesses to our flak jackets. I put mine on and stepped to the mirror. It was cool seeing myself in my flak jacket, with my military haircut and dead-serious look on my face. Mom and Dad wouldn't recognize me. I feel like a real Marine.

MONDAY, MAY 15: TD-42

Today is the first official day of A-LINE. A-LINE is the next level of training, where we will be familiarized with many different types of weaponry. For example, the M-60 and M249 SAW machine guns, the M203 grenade launcher, and the AT-4 missile launcher. We'll also do some more M16 firing, learning some new methods of engagement, including a night fire.

Right now you'd think we would be more pumped up, but ever since we'd moved into building #761 (a.k.a. the White Elephant – it's been around since the WWII era), Platoon 1082 has been down in the dumps, motivation-wise. It's about 96 degrees out, hot enough to merit the black flag (which flies to warn of excessive heat, signifying a non-physical training day). We got our flag/guidon rolled up like a tampon, and we're tired and feeling pretty beat-up. One thing that does motivate us, surprisingly enough, is the Port-O-Johns. Inside those nasty, dirty crappers is some great graffiti – left by recruits in our same exact training phase:

"15 and a wake-up, and I'm off this MF-ing Island!"

"This is my crap. There are many like it but this one is mine."

"15 days and a pit call to go!"

"14 and a bowl of cereal to go!"

All through Boot Camp, you don't have to keep track of time – you just have to check the proper shitter. These shitters were telling me to wake the hell up, to suck it up, and realize how close I was to graduating as a UNITED STATES MARINE!

Today, in classes, recruits were falling asleep like crazy. Even our squad leader can't stay awake – Recruit Martin and I took turns throwing cold water in his face. By this time, everyone had made up his own little motivational countdown calendars. It's not the right thing to do, kind of like keeping score during your practice rounds at the range, but everyone does it. Recruit Stillwell got caught looking at his "high-tech" calendar watch by the Senior. We thought he was going to thrash him, or all of us, but he just gave this look of disgust, which hurt us even more. At lunch, SDI Bixby gave us a lecture on our noticeable decline in motivation.

"YOU'RE NEARING THE END OF TRAINING, AND I CAN'T UNDERSTAND FOR THE LIFE OF ME WHY YOU RECRUITS ARE

LOSING MOTIVATION! FROM NOW ON, UNTIL YOU START SHOWING ME YOU GIVE A SHIT, I DON'T GIVE A SHIT! IF YOU'RE NOT GOING TO GIVE 110% FOR ME, THEN BY GOD, YOU ARE NOT GOING TO GET THE 200%, MY DRILL INSTRUCTORS AND I HAVE BEEN GIVING TO YOU!"

He's totally right. He has been looking out for us since Training Day -1, and we don't always do all we could to deserve it. Sure it's his job and all, but we came to him, not the other way around. DI Wight gave us the same speech only a few days ago, but the message is driven home so much more harshly when given by the Senior.

On the rifle range today, I shot 10 rounds in groups of 3, 3, and 4 from the 36-yard line. My first three shots were off to the left, so I adjusted my sight. The next three were low and just right. I made another sight adjustment, when the instructor, a corporal, bet me 20 push-ups for each shot that fell outside the bulls-eye. I knew it wasn't really a bet, and 4 x 20 was 80 push-ups, which I didn't feel like doing since I was already sweating my cahones off. Still, the pressure was just what I needed. All four shots – BAM – were in the bull's eye. No push-ups – Recruit Price was saved!

Next, we fired in quickly assumed positions. We had never really done these exercises before, like magazine changes and immediate actions for rifle jams. This time, the Marine in charge was an overweight lance corporal. I'll never forget this prick. His name was Willis.

Willis kept asking me, "ARE YOU A SHITBIRD, RECRUIT PRICE?"

To call this pudgeball "sir" hurt me, but I responded "No, Sir." He just kept after me, making 20 minutes seem like two hours. "LET'S GO, SHITBIRD!! HURRY UP, COME ON SHITBIRD! CAN'T YOU DO ANYTHING RIGHT?"

When the day was over, I found out he gave the same treatment to Recruits Martin and O'Donnell, rushing them through the exercises as well. I really don't like him.

This evening I had a record six letters – two were from Kimball. After mail call, we had a mock Gong Show with SDI Bixby. It wasn't really the most appropriate time for it, but it produced some laughs anyway. I did my imitations of SSgt. Ciprioni and Recruit Lish, and got a good laugh. He asked us if everything went all right today and we knew this was our chance to tell him about that prick lance corporal. Basically, this is called "dropping the dime" on him, but telling our Senior such things is the only means of defense we have.

Senior told us not to worry about any of the lance corporals working the ranges. "A lot of them are rejects and broke dicks that couldn't make it into the FMF (the Fleet Marine Force, a.k.a. "The Marines"). They know it, the Drill Instructors know it, and now *you* know it. When they call you a shitbird, they are really calling *themselves* shitbirds. O'Donell, Martin and I looked at each other, and we felt a lot better.

TUESDAY, MAY 16: TD-43

At 0400 this morning, 1082 got a wake-up call, weapons training style. SDI Bixby is still highly displeased with our lack of motivation. He said we are singing like a bunch of bitches when we answer him or sound off. He's right, too. We can't seem to help it. Everyone has their eyes on the prize – the title United States Marine – but our concentration is way off. In First Phase, everyone was locked-on. Yes, we were counting the days, but you don't really get distracted by days when you've got 60 left. Now we're in Third Phase, count down mode, and it's hurting our focus. I know it's true, because I'm guilty of it myself.

Today was another friggin' boiling hot day, plus we had to wear our flak jackets and helmets all day. We were sweating buckets. On the range, we shot limited rounds while engaging multiple targets and moving targets. The best part was definitely shooting at the moving targets. All in all, we fired 104 rounds.

By the afternoon, we were down in the butts again. We broke down into three-man teams. It was Mulroy, Hockenberry and myself. As you may recall, Hockenberry is one of the guys whose leg was hurt. He skated through BWT while we were all busting our asses, and we heard that he was bragging about how he was getting away with murder. Big mistake.

The hardest job was to carry the target on a stick back and forth while the shooters fired on it. I don't know if he thought there was going to be a vote or a picking of the longest straw, but we ended those ideas quickly. It hardly had to do with his leg injury so I told him, "Hockenberry, get your ass on that target and start paying your dues!"

On top of having to hold it up forever, he had to keep his flak and helmet on and wear a set of goggles. He was frying his ass off, while our sweat-drenched cammies were starting to dry off. He kept asking to switch out, but Mulroy kept telling him to shut his man-pleaser and do his job. We told him we heard how he was bragging about skating, while we were getting killed at BWT. "The party's over, freak, you better wake up and start busting your ass, or your next lesson is gonna come from the Senior!" After our little talk, he did start stepping it up. "A miracle – *not.*"

Bad news on the Collins saga. As I feared, his leg is not getting better, and he's being sent to MRP (Medical Reconditioning Platoon) to join Recruit Donner. To be this close to graduation and not make it would kill me. Collins' situation reminded me of a football field goal kicker who's called on to kick the winner with only seconds left. Everyone stays away from him, and doesn't say a word. I've tried to talk to him, but what do you say? It's like a funeral. There's just nothing to say. Recruit Hockenberry is doing a lot better – he'll probably be able to finish CCC in time. The BMC or Base Medical Center told him he'd better or it's MRP – that combined with our talk was all the inspiration he needed.

During breaks in our A-LINE classes, we fill our canteens or make head calls. It is so hot out, that if water either going in your body or it is leaving it! Twice I got "stage-fright" in the head, and couldn't piss. Why? Because some DIs from 1080 were banging the Port-O-John and shaking it while screaming, "PISS! PISS! PISS!" After the pleasantry of being shaken in a shitter like a mixed drink, I started to sneak all my leaks, or at least make sure the coast was clear.

Tonight's night-fire on the range was awesome – like something out of the movie "Platoon" or even "Star Wars." We fired pretty much the same course as in the daytime, only we did it with tracer rounds. They helped us see where our rounds were impacting. Illumination grenades with parachutes were being shot overhead to give us more light and to help silhouette the targets. The overall effect of it was even greater

During A-Line, one of the weapons we got to fire was the M16A2 Service Rifle affixed with M203 Grenade Launcher. We also fired the M-249 SAW machine gun.

when we were back in the butts. From that angle, it seemed like World War III had broken out. Hundreds of red flashes were blasting through the targets and disappearing into the treeline, and the 'illum' rounds were casting some very ominous shadows all around us. All in all, it was a great night... an event I could have never experienced had I remained a civilian.

WEDNESDAY, MAY 17: TD-44

We woke up late at 0530. I put on my cammies from the night before. They were still kind of damp from all the sweat they had soaked up, plus it's only 0600 and already the temperature is in the 90s. We headed to chow. I found out that if you lose 30 pounds during boot camp, you get rewarded by being given five sets of cammies for free!

Now I have an extra incentive to lose another ten pounds. Breakfast was three small boxes of cereal, eggs, a piece of melon – skipped the doughnut. On the way back from chow, our squad leader got caught scratching. Damn sand fleas.

"WHERE DOES IT ITCH? WHERE DOES IT ITCH?? YOU NASTY LITTLE UNDISCIPLINED THING YOU!" Butler roared. "WELL THEN, START SCRATCHING... HARDER.... HARDER!"

Butler made our squad leader scratch all day long as punishment. I don't think he'll be scratching again anytime soon!

In morning class, we learned about two highly powerful weapons. Everyone was a little awe-struck, but part of being a Marine Recruit and maintaining your military bearing is not showing emotion. Sergeant Hopkins came in the room holding an M203 grenade launcher. It is actually an M16A2 service rifle with the capabilities to shoot grenades added in. The sergeant was a big boy, and the stance in which he held the weapon was pretty doggone intimidating.

"THE SAFETY ON MY OLD WEAPON KEPT GETTING STUCK, SO THE ARMORER GOT ME A NEW ONE! THIS IS ONE **BITCHIN'** PIECE OF GEAR, SO LISTEN UP AND GET READY TO LEARN!"

The whole room boomed back, "YES SIR!" Then, we learned all about the M203 grenade launcher. It's weight, ranges, and the types of grenades it could fire. The M203 is good to go!

Then Sgt. Hopkins gave us a five-minute breather to "SHAKE THE

DEW OFF YOUR LILIES," and stretch out. So, we did our usual, packing two at a time in the port o' potties to make sure the DIs didn't shake the hell out of us, or we found little hiding spots to pee. Then, we were right back in the classroom. This time our instructor brought out an AT-4 (Anti-Tank 4th Generation).

This is a bazooka, for all you nasty civilians out there. It has a maximum effective range of 400 meters and the impact packs quite a punch, we were told. The part I found interesting is that once you fire the weapon, the AT-4 is then discarded, adding further to the Marine creed: "One shot, one kill."

After the classes were over, we moved on to the unknown distance course. We were shown four different areas from which we would be engaging targets. From the four main "covered" positions (before we fired, we had to insure we had proper cover or shielding from enemy fire), we shot at B-Mod targets.

Some of the targets weren't too far away, but there were some that were out there, to say the least. When we hit a target, it would fall down – pretty awesome. It was better than any video game I ever played.

We also fired practice rounds out of the AT-4. Our target was a beat-up old tank about 350 yards away. Since the AT-4 costs around $800 a pop, and once fired it is worthless, the Marine Corps has training AT-4s from which you can fire 9mm tracer rounds.

This is to help you get comfortable with the sights and elevation dial before you fire the real deal. We got to fire ten rounds apiece. It was fun firing at the tank, and wondering what it would be like if it was a real missile.

Lunch was a bag nasty. We quickly scarfed it down, and were introduced to our next instructor, a tall, lanky guy who looked kind of goofy, not like most of the instructors we had met. He told us some stories about his MOS or job. He was a sniper and he told us he had won many awards for his marksmanship. It made me wonder. All these Marines have such awesome abilities. Where will I fit in?

He gave our platoon a period of instruction on the M60 and M249 SAW machine guns. He said we wouldn't really get into the M60, since it was being phased out by the Corps. We would focus on the M249 SAW.

Its maximum effective range is 1100 meters. It weighs only 15 pounds, but it can fire up to 750 rounds a minute!

He broke it down for us, showed us how to put it back together, and we practiced loading belts of dummy rounds. He told us that we'd be firing today. Fifty round belts a piece, but if he could arrange it, we might be able to fire more. Good looking out, Sir, I thought to myself.

Well, we only got a 50-round belt each, and yeah, it went quickly – but wow, was it powerful! We were in a fighting hole, with our A-gunner to help get us on target, but truthfully, I was just letting the rounds fly and loving it. I fired 6-8 round bursts for the first half of my rounds and then our main instructor (the sniper) came over and told me, "GET SOME! GET SOME! FINISH IT!" So I did what any obedient recruit would do, I fired off a 25-round burst. It was great, only like I said, it went too quickly.

Next, we moved over to the M203 grenade launcher range. There was a big hunk of rusted metal the size of a mini-bus about 250 meters away. That was our point of aim. We each got two inert or practice rounds, and took aim. My first was about 50 meters long – way off. Then I made an elevation adjustment and smacked my second one right off the side of it. Overall, only six out of 50 of us hit, so I felt pretty good about that.

Our instructor told us we did a good job today. Then came "Police Call!" "IF IT DON'T GROW, IT'S GOT TO GO!" So we policed up our range, picking up everything that wasn't alive, and tossed it in the garbage.

It's Wednesday, so after that we marched from the range to the barbershop for our sixth and final recruit baldy haircut. We were running late, so we practically ran to get to the barbershop. It's been so friggin' hot out, we were happy to get haircuts just to cool our domes off – but it's a relief to know that it's the last one. From now on, the tops of our grapes are off-limits to those barbers. Nothing personal, but it's rough on us when they buzz all 50 of us in about a half-hour, 30 seconds each. They're fast, but a little lacking in the compassion department. Those clippers cut hard and viciously. One of our knuckleheads has a mole on the back of his head that gets cut open every time. He finally got the guts up to say something to the barber. Next week is the long-awaited and famous Marine high-and-tight, given only to Third Phase Recruits near graduation. Can't wait!

On the way from the barbershop, heading toward the white elephants, something sad happened. We passed Recruit Collins, walking by on a pair of crutches. DI Parks stopped us in our tracks and told us, "I want you recruits to yell 'We'll miss you, Recruit Collins.' "

"WE'LL MISS YOU, RECRUIT COLLINS," 1082 shouted to him.

He looked at us, as he raised his crutch and replied, "CARRY ON, RECRUITS!"

I could feel a tear coming. It's easy to lose a shit-bird from the platoon, but Collins is a good guy. I had never really asked him how he was feeling, but when we got back to the squad bay, I found his letter to the platoon on my rack.

> To Plt. 1082: I can't believe I'm getting sent to MRP. So close, yet so far! I'm doing everything I can to hold in my emotions, but I've never felt like this before. I feel like I've failed, but I know I haven't. I feel like I've lost the game, but it all depends on how you look at it. I'm going to be lifting weights, swimming, and getting healthy — someday I will be a Marine. Everyone in 1082 deserves a big OOH-RAH for being the biggest ass-kicking, pavement-pounding, stick-beating, face-smashing MOTHERF'ERS in Lead Series! Hope your careers as Marines are everything you want and more. Take care of yourselves. Semper Fidelis! — Recruit Collins

I give Collins a lot of credit for how he's handling his situation. He's been sentenced to eight more weeks (minimum) on The Island. It must have hurt him deeply to know that he will not graduate with Platoon 1082.

In a letter, I was notified that my mother's aunt – my great aunt – is very sick, so tonight I left the squad bay with a walking chit to make an emergency phone call to her. When I spoke to my mother, she told me that our aunt wasn't as bad as everyone had feared. So we talked and she told me this was a bad way to get to hear from me, but she was glad to hear my voice. She also told me how she couldn't wait to see me. It was good to hear her voice and know that she is proud of me. After we hung up, I couldn't resist. I sneaked in a quick call to Kimball.

"Holy shit!" he yelled, when he realized it was me, "It's Recruit Price! How's it going buddy?"

"Good," I told him.

"I know. I can tell by your letters. Do you like it?"

"Yes, I like it."

"You sound different. More sure of yourself."

"I am different," I told him, "Listen, I've got to go. Just wanted to say hi from Parris Island."

"Keep up the good work, Will! I'm proud of you. See you soon."

It sounded strange to hear someone calling me by my first name after so long. I'd forgotten I had one. Walking back to the squad bay, I was just outside the window, when I heard Platoon 1082 sounding off. It felt weird to hear the rest of the platoon sounding off without me. It made me want to be with them, no matter what – for better or worse. That's just a fraction of what Collins must be feeling. But as always, things move so fast here you can't dwell on trash like this. Too much focusing on the past and you become the past yourself. However, Platoon 1082 will not forget you, Recruit Collins.

THURSDAY, MAY 18: TD-45

I had fire watch duty between 0200-0300 this morning, and then got up at 0400. Recruit Snedeker, stuffing his ALICE pack with gear and knocking into my rack, interrupted my brief hour of sleep. I remember I was having an awesome dream. I wanted to kill him for waking me. But, Recruit Price is ready to attack the last day of A-LINE instead, minus two hours of sleep. We're now getting our last classes that combine – "Moving Targets" and "Firing with a Gas Mask On." The air-conditioning is kicking in, making everyone sleepier than we already are.

After class, we fired at the moving targets – another installment of the best video game I have ever played. Next, we fired with gas masks on. Talk about sweating your ass off. If I ever have to go to a war where they're using chemical warfare, I'm going to melt before the enemy has a chance to shoot me.

Tempers are flaring in this heat. Recruits Pechette and Paventi just got into a fight for no good reason. When Paventi told Pechette to take his diapers off and quit crying, he about lost it and we had to break it up before the DIs saw. I've also been a little on edge with my fellow recruits (i.e. Recruit Snedeker this morning). After living with 50-plus Marine Recruits for two months, you naturally start to go a little loco.

When we got back to the Basic Warriors Training area, we immediately piled off the bus and started putting up our hooches. We are back to complete BWT testing, which includes a variety of knowledge tests, and to negotiate the Combat Assault Course. Recruit Mulroy and I teamed up for the night. He's a good guy – an MP reservist looking to become a cop. We've been pow-wowing all evening, testing each other on our knowledge and doing crunches.

Tonight SDI Bixby sat us all down before lights out. He's the best. He told us how a recruit from his last platoon got dropped. Whenever we do any type of physical activity, we have to empty our pockets – this knucklehead didn't. He left his ink-stick (pen) in his pocket, and while he was negotiating the course by low-crawling and diving, he stabbed himself. Good to go, idiot.

The last night of BWT is known as "Warrior's Night," where we light a big fire and tell stories. It's also a night for mischief. For some reason, we were not allowed to have the fire, but our Senior had no problem authorizing the mischief part. SDI Bixby sent out a "commando squad," with orders to "reappropriate" some helmets and to collapse a couple of hooches from Platoon 1080. Mission accepted. Mulroy and I had already hinted to SDI Bixby that we hoped he would let us loose on the other platoons during our 0200-0300 fire watch. Just let us loose! When it started to get dark, SDI Bixby came to our hooch and cleared us hot for 0200.

We closed the night with this chant for SDI Bixby: "SIR, COUNT ON DECK IS 50 HIGHLY MOTIVATED, TRULY DEDICATED, ROUGH-TOUGH CAN'T GET ENOUGH, TWISTED OF STEEL WITH A WHOLE LOT OF SEX APPEAL, UNITED STATES MARINE RECRUITS, SIR!"

We kind of messed it up, not saying it all in rhythm, and a couple of 1080's big mouth recruits started rubbing our faces in it. We were pissed, but happy. Now we had more reason to target them for tonight's mission.

At 0145, we were awakened for our fire watch/destruction raid. We didn't really find any loose gear ripe for the taking and their fire watch was staying real close to their guidons, but that left their hooches unguarded. So, we started to put all our training in night movement and stealth to the test. We low-crawled up to the hooch that had the two big-mouthed recruits in it. We took four of their stakes completely out of the ground and loosened the remaining ones leaving their hooch totally unstable. Then we tied about 30 yards of 550 cord to the top of the hooch leading it in the direction of the third platoon in the area. We got far enough away and I sent Mulroy back on his watch. Then, I yanked at the cord as hard as I could, collapsing their hooch all over them. I don't know how I didn't burst out laughing when I heard them cursing and bitching up a storm. Mulroy said he could see them trying to fight their way out of the hooch.

The next morning, as if things couldn't get better, we found out that 1080 was getting a wake-up pit call for waking their DIs up. They had figured it was Platoon 1081 that did it because of where the cord led. They declared war on 1081, only they caused quite a ruckus in doing so. We told our Senior what happened and he laughed. I think we are starting to get back on his good side as a platoon. Overall, our mission was declared a success!

FRIDAY, MAY 19: TD-46

Back home at 1st Battalion again. Good to be back in our old squad bay, kicking it on our hour of free time. We've even got the A/C blasting. BWT testing today was no problemo. We were tested on everything from donning and clearing our gas masks, to all the different types of weapons and grenades, to first aid. We were very prepared, to say the least.

The hardest part was the Combat Assault Course. It was really tiring. We hit the course four recruits at a time, on four different trails. It was non-stop, low-crawling under barbed wire with 1/4 pound sticks of TNT blowing up all around us, smoke grenades going off, and simulated loud, gruesome death-screams booming from speakers. We had to climb over walls, and negotiate some barbwire as best we could. When that was done, we were told to fix our bayonets to our weapons and assault the "Jacki the Iraqi" dummies, giving two vicious deathblows a piece. Next, we were given several practice grenades to throw at the enemy, then we were done. Writing about it now, it doesn't sound as hard as it really was, but boy I was winded.

Afterward, we were tasked with raking and fixing up the course for the next recruits, who are to take it in a week or so. Our job was interrupted by a kick-ass thunder and lightning storm. Not only did it interrupt our little working party, but it also had the DIs talking about how we might have to take a bus back to 1st battalion. This, as opposed to a 10-mile hump back to the rear, would have been great. As luck would have it, the storm blew past in typical South Carolina fashion, and we lined up for the march. On the way, we passed by a bunch of First Phasers on Training Day 4. They were all disoriented and scared shitless. It was funny watching them practically tripping over their own feet. To think that was once *me!*

After we were back, all showered and shaved, I ran to the scale to see where my fat body was at. I am down to an unbelievable 189 pounds. Physically, I've never felt better. Mentally, I am no longer the confused, directionless kid I was when I was "back on the block," or even back when I was standing on those yellow footprints.

During our free time, I saw the uniform I'll be wearing at graduation, complete with a chevron on the sleeve. This was to make sure that the recruits who are guaranteed the rank of Private First Class have the rank on their shoulder. One chevron indicates a PFC. This may not seem like a big deal, but trust me, it is, especially if you don't *have* that chevron. Things are finally starting to come together. Just two more weeks and we will be part of the few and the proud.

SDI Bixby told us a while ago that there would be three meritorious promotions given by him. Tonight, he chose Recruits Hill, Bates, and Paventi. Paventi had better thank fate. Only a few days ago, that promotion belonged to Collins.

After free time, something pretty funny happened. DI Parks was going down the line performing nightly hygiene inspection. If we are not completely silent during the inspection, he flips the hell out. Well, picture all of us recruits in our BVDs, skivvy shirts and flip-flops. Our scribe, the recruit that writes down all our discrepancies, is following Parks. Only tonight, he decides it would be funny to give himself a wedgie. He hiked his tighty-whiteys so far up his ass, he looked like a doggone sumo wrestler! By some kind of miracle, we managed to hold back our laughter.

SATURDAY, MAY 20: TD-47

We woke up at 0400 and did our usual PT and three-mile run. About halfway into the run, SDI Bixby decided to unfurl our Platoon guidon. I didn't realize how much seeing it would mean to me, but when I saw it flying at the front of the platoon, I got an incredible rush of excitement. We all started screaming OOH-RAH, and kept on yelling the whole rest of the way. Platoon 1082 is back! Afterward, we drilled.

"YOU DID BETTER THAN I EXPECTED," SDI Bixby told us, "BUT YOU STILL SUCKED!"

Recruit Rivera got his ass reamed by Bixby, and Recruit Shales almost got his fingers broken by DI Wight for not keeping them curled. This week is going to be Shales' worst nightmare. He's terrible at drill. He turns into a disaster area when the pressure is on, and *it is on.*

Later, we fixed our graduation blouses, adding a badge and National Defense Ribbon for the Marines fighting overseas. As we were sizing our trousers, I was fidgeting with the waistline. DI Parks told us all to stop messing with them until he got there. I was kind of unhappy with the fit, so I just kept on making adjustments. I didn't ignore him on purpose. I suppose I was just "in a zone" or something. I didn't even notice that he was only one recruit away from me. Then I saw the look on his face. He was pissed.

"YOU GOIN' SOMEWHERE RECRUIT?" he shouted. Then he punched me right in the chest.

Before you join up, the recruiters tell you DIs aren't allowed to hit the recruits, ever – but since I've come here, I've noticed that "ever" can be a mighty short time. If and when it happens, it is never done to cause physical pain – it is much more mental. They seem to know exactly whom they can hit, also. They tend to go after recruits like me, who they know will never make a complaint against them. And I wouldn't! I respect most of them too much. Besides, sometimes I deserve a good slug to set me straight. After he slugged me, I was mad, but more embarrassed than anything. To make matters worse, I looked up and saw Landers, the recruit across from me, with this big shit-eating grin on his face. I was furious. I couldn't hold back.

"WHAT THE F--- IS SO FUNNY, LANDERS??"

I watched very happily as DI Parks got right in Landers' face. Deep down I wanted him to see him slug Landers.

"WHAT IS SO FRIGGIN' FUNNY, LANDERS?"

"Nothing sir." As DI Parks stormed back to inspecting our blues' trousers, I could see Landers wasn't laughing anymore.

After chow, I played a joke on some of the guys and especially Landers – more evidence of my new Third Phase attitude. I left the chow hall a little before they did and waited outside. As they all came rushing out, I stepped back into them with my head down and screamed in my best imitation DI voice, "GET OUT OF THE WAY!" They all jumped and froze at attention. Recruit Landers almost flew out of his skin. It was a riot watching the confused look on his face, because he didn't know which way to go around me. I laughed hysterically for nearly five minutes.

On the way back to the squad bay, we asked DI Parks if we could do some "motivating drill" for the new recruits in the area. To our surprise, he said okay. We waited until we found some First Phasers passing by and DI Parks started to chant to them and us, "IF YOU LIKE YOUR BOOTY TIGHT, STOMP YOUR LEFT AND DRAG YOUR RIGHT!"

The platoon, as we had been coached, promptly stomped with the left and dragged our right boots, singing the response, "SEX COSTS MONEY! SEX COSTS MONEY!" As we did it, we didn't need to see them to know that they were in awe of us, and that we were looking good. Our Company Executive Officer passed by as we were chanting, and started laughing. He liked that trash.

That night, during hygiene inspection, DI Parks ripped into some recruits for their rotten, stinking skivvies (underwear) – an endless source of amusement. Oh, and our scribe was also back to his old tricks. This time, while he was doing the sumo wrestler bit, our Company Commander just happened to be strolling by the back hatch. We never saw him, but he sure saw Martin. "WHAT IN GOD'S NAME DO YOU THINK YOU'RE DOING, RECRUIT??"

Martin's jaw hit the floor. Then I think DI Parks's jaw joined him. He told the CO, "THANK YOU SIR. I THINK I CAN HANDLE IT FROM HERE."

"VERY WELL SERGEANT, CARRY ON!"

"AYE SIR!" And then it was on.

"NOT ONLY DO YOU NOT ANNOUNCE THE COMPANY COMMANDER ON DECK, BUT YOU WANT TO PLAY GAMES BEHIND THE DRILL INSTRUCTOR'S BACK! I HAVE NEVER BEEN SO EMBARRASSED IN MY STINKIN' LIFE. GOOD TO GO. YOU LITTLE RECRUITS WANT TO PLAY GAMES, WELL WE'RE GONNA PLAY SOME FRIGGIN' GAMES NOW!"

The first thing he did was have us all pull our skivvies up our ass, until they couldn't go a millimeter further. Then he had us perform our clean up, thrashed us for about a good half-hour, and put us into the racks still with our wedgies. What a sight we were.

All in all, we're pretty busy campers. Inspections, drills, and PT – just 12 days and a wake-up to graduation. I just hope we don't have any more nights like this one again.

SUNDAY, MAY 21

It's God day, and Platoon 1082 spent all four hours of our free time preparing for the Company Commander's Inspection tomorrow. Cleaning rifles, shining shoes, clipping off Irish pennants (loose threads), and the big moment: Recruit Price put on his service Alphas and cover (inspection uniform and hat) for the first time! I never knew olive drab was my color until now. My uniform looks and feels fantastic. I can't wait to wear it, and be seen by the world. For a minute I was worried I wouldn't be ready for inspection, but now, I know I *am* ready. It's going to be rocking tomorrow when I get to wear my Alphas officially for the first time.

Staring in the mirror, in my perfectly pressed service Alphas and new barracks cover, I almost didn't recognize myself. I looked like a military man. Then it occurred to me that that's what I AM now. When we changed from service Alphas, back to cammies – the uniforms we wear every day – they had my nametag, PRICE, sewn on the pocket. Another sign that the end is in sight. Soon, soon, soon, we will join the few and the proud. OOH-RAH! We're so close that we can hardly believe it. After all this time, 11 days just seems TOO close.

We're all getting really pumped up – and the more pumped we are, the cooler our DIs are. They love seeing us totally motivated and ready to go. We're finally being treated like men and not "maggots." SDI Bixby even gave me back the "contraband" camera that Kimball sent me a month ago. He told me "YOU BETTER NOT LET ME *CATCH YOU* TAKING PICTURES WITH THIS, PRICE!" Translation: Don't get caught! (Can you guess where that picture of me and my rifle on the front cover of this book, and also on the next page, came from?)

There are three types of people in this world. The first type is born with a plan, and from day one they have everything all figured out. But they always wonder what might have happened if they had chosen another road. The second type are those who just let life take them where it wants. They wind up in some shitty job, and always wonder how they would have been if they had planned better – usually over a few beers. This was the type Recruit Price *used* to be.

The third type are those who get tired with letting life take them where it wants, and decide to choose their *own* path. In spite of criticism from others who are jealous, or have never found the courage to take charge of their own lives, this type dares to throw away his past and takes risks shooting for something better. This is the type I have become as a Marine Recruit. I have stepped up to the challenge. Next stop, the world!

MONDAY, MAY 22: TD-48

The day of reckoning arrived – and it wasn't so bad. All the work that goes into preparing for inspection is mind-boggling when you consider that the whole thing only takes about a minute. A few recruits did not pass muster. Capt. Stopa, the friggin' huge and intimidating as hell Marine who inspected us, went off on Recruits Stilwell and Medina. They *still* didn't know their general orders.

"NO MARINE GETS OFF MY ISLAND WITHOUT KNOWING HIS GENERAL ORDERS!" Capt. Stopa roared in their faces.

Another recruit failed for having rust on his rifle – a serious offense in the fleet. If the three lagging recruits don't pass tomorrow, it's curtains for them. Considering that Stilwell failed knowledge testing twice and Medina "No hablas Ingles" very well, they should be worried.

With the "smuggled" camera (the SDI returned it to me at the end of bootcamp), I was able to capture this image during my firewatch on the last day before we turned in our rifles to the armory for good.

We spent the rest of the day getting re-fitted for our uniforms, because a lot of them were sized wrong. Then we marched off to chow in smaller, individual groups. Part of the privileges of being a Third Phase Recruit is getting more freedom – but not *that* much. We're still just "maggots" until graduation. At lunch chow, I saw Recruit Collins. He came over and we shook hands and talked for a couple of minutes. He's trying to keep his strength and spirits up, but it was easy for me to see that MRP (Medical Reconditioning Platoon) is killing him. My heart really goes out to him.

After lunch it was drill and more drill. That night, SDI Bixby was on duty during my fire watch. We talked for about half an hour. He told me that when I get in the fleet and I go overseas, I should bring a case of Zippo lighters with me, because in some countries you can trade them for all kinds of treasure. In Turkey, you can get leather goods, and in Israel it's diamonds. He said in the Philippines, food, beer and women are el cheapo, and warned me that in foreign countries, I'd better stay out of trouble. Another day passed. Lights out! Tomorrow, it's eight days and a wake-up.

TUESDAY, MAY 23: TD-49

Currently, this is the day when recruits begin the training period known as "The Crucible." When I attended bootcamp, I did similar exercises, a little earlier, during Basic Warrior Training. Named after the vessel used to create steel, The Crucible is intended to forge Marines out of raw recruits.

It begins on Tuesday of Week 10 with a 6-mile hike to Parks Field, a huge landing strip that runs for miles. The entire Crucible , which lasts 54 hours, tests recruits on their abilities to work together as a team, while dealing with the stresses of sleep and food deprivation. The training focuses on leadership and team-building exercises, while honing recruits' infantry skills.

The amount of sleep is limited to just 6-10 hours. There are four main exercises, and a variety of secondary. In between exercises, recruits march up to two miles to reach their next testing area. When The Crucible ends, the platoons are mobilized for a 9-mile hike, at zero-dark-thirty, back to their battalion areas for the Warrior's Breakfast.

They're allowed enough time to lock up their weapons and wash the cammie paint off their mugs, then it's off to chowhall for a complete hour of chow, with multiple repeat visits allowed. During the breakfast, each recruit receives an "Honor, Courage and Commitment" card. Now their final week of bootcamp begins and recruits are treated less like recruits and more like Marines.

But getting back to MY story...

As usual, another 0500 wake-up, and as usual, we sounded off – but today was extra LOUD. Must be graduation nearing. We did our usual PT, then some drill. Drill went pretty good today, and we're showing some improvement. The only problem was with Recruit Lindsay. The firing pin retaining pin on his rifle was missing, and it got noticed. SDI Bixby was pissed. Apparently, SDI Bixby is responsible for every last detail of our weapons, and this one would cost him some embarrassment.

"I'M GONNA GET YOU, LINDSAY!" he told him.

They videotaped us today for the Platoon video. I wonder if they got that little comment on tape. When we got back to First Battalion, I asked Lindsay, "Do you still have your BRAIN retaining pin?" He was pissed at me, but everybody else laughed. He deserved it.

This afternoon, I finally got to tackle the Confidence Course. At last! No description of Marine basic training would be complete without it. For the first time on the course, I thought I did pretty well, but DI Wight didn't agree with me. He said I came up short on the triceps-walk and overhead monkey swing.

The A Ladder is a bit scary. It is a 20-foot rope climb, then a 20-foot ladder climb to a rope hanging three feet away from your reach. You have to lunge for it, staying confident, that you will be safe and just grab hold. Then, you've got to monkey down on the rope vertically. I did it, no problem.

I also did the infamous Slide For Life like a pro. You have to lay on top of a rope which slants downward at about a 40-degree angle.

You've got to use it to cross over a pool of water 40 feet below. If you fall, you have got to come out of the water with your hands on your head, singing the Marines' Hymn! On another Confidence Course obstacle, recruits have to work together to scale a series of elevated platforms. Our DIs do all these obstacles right along with us, and it was just my luck to have DI Wight in back of me for this one. I climbed up the first platform, and he screamed at me.

"GIVE ME YOUR HAND!"

I extended my hand and then I grabbed his arm. Suddenly he started freaking.

"LET GO OF ME! PRICE! LET GO OF ME NOW!"

I was taken aback, because I had only done what he told me to. I released his hand.

"GRAB ME PRICE, GRAB ME!" he shouted again.

Now, I lost my military bearing in the worst way. "What the F---, SIR?" I yelled at Wight.

He exploded. "WHO THE F--- DO YOU THINK YOU'RE TALKING TO, RECRUIT?"

I didn't back down. "Sir, you TOLD ME to grab you! I did, then you told me to LET YOU GO!"

He started to shout back at me, but I could tell that he respected my anger as being somewhat justified. Luckily, SDI Bixby came along, and found the situation funny. That calmed us both down. Later some recruits even gave me a pat on the back for standing up to DI Wight.

This afternoon was another big symbolic event. We marched to the barbershop for our first high-and-tight haircut. We waited in line as usual, but this time all excited that we were finally going to be allowed to keep the hair on the tops of our grapes intact. And, after a quick and brutal as usual buzz, the job was done.

It was sort of anti-climactic, because we just got our last Recruit cuts a week ago and our tops hadn't really grown out that much. I'm still pretty friggin' bald. Nevertheless, it felt great. Hopefully

Recruit Price with his first official "High and Tight!" Do I look like a Jarhead yet?

the next H & T, our last Parris Island haircut, will look better. Now it's time to rack out. Eight days and a wake-up!

WEDNESDAY, MAY 24: TD-50

We had our last Table PT session today. OOH-RAH! I thought for sure the Series Gunny was going to tear us all new assholes, but he only pained us a little. Maybe because we did a four-mile run instead of our usual three. It was no problem for me – once I get going, I feel like I could keep on running for at least ten miles. Then we drilled some more. It's hard to keep your mind on drill, especially now that when we go to classes, real Marines are talking to us like we are semi-equals. The Master Sergeant who gave us a class on Recruiter's Assistance was a riot. Hearing him talk and bust our balls with all that Marine slang lingo was great – I can't wait to master all that trash myself.

In another class, everyone got their orders for either MCT (Marine Combat Training) or SOI (School Of Infantry). Pretty exciting. We also looked over our SRBs (Service Record Books). It's all so official. They also took the pictures that will go on our military ID cards. I look like one mean mo-fo in that shot – reminded me of the awful mug shot they took of me in jail. But this time I'm on the side of the good guys.

Before racking out, we chanted, "HIGH-LEEEE MOTIVATED, TRU-LEEEE DEDICATED! WE ARE ROUGH, WE ARE TOUGH, WE CAN'T GET ENOUGH! TWISTED OF STEEL, WITH A WHOLE LOT OF SEX APPEAL, GRADUATING IN ONE WEEK, UNITED STATES MARINE CORPS RECRUITS!"

Right now it's about 0435 and I am making a sitting head call. We have to wake up soon. So tired. Graduation nears – I can't wait to get some degree of freedom back in my life.

THURSDAY, MAY 25: TD-51

Before joining the Marines, I tried being a substitute teacher. When there was nothing to do, I made up "busy work" just to keep the class occupied. That is what today was like. We drilled (again) and did a mock PFT (Physical Fitness Test). Recruit Price did 14 pull-ups, 84 sit-ups and ran 3 miles in 20 minutes 45 seconds. Good to go! The real PFT is this coming Monday. In the afternoon we spit-shined our boots and were given a Personal Assistance class by Cpl. Yi – a real nice guy. We got our final drill cards today, the ones that tell us exactly what movements we'll have to perform for Final Drill inspection. Six days and a wake-up.

FRIDAY, MAY 26: TD-52

We are having our final period of drill practice. We've drilled so much that if we don't pull it together for final drill tomorrow it will be a real tragedy. SDI Bixby has promised us a pizza party if we win the drill competition. Right about now, I could go for a nice fat slice.

Today Recruit DeAngelis, a would-be Miami mobster, went to sick call with a hurt leg. He returned with a huge bandage on his knee. He's got until Monday to get better. If he can't pass the PFT, especially the three-mile run, he's gone. Can you imagine getting dropped on TD-52?! Give me a friggin' break!

This afternoon we got our first paychecks. Yes, we are actually getting *paid* to do this torture – a whopping $1,332. Not much for three months, but it's a start. Considering I had forgotten we were "working" the whole time I was here, I should be grateful for every penny. I thought this final week would be pretty intense and heavy on the pit calls, but it's actually been pretty lax so far. Today, besides drilling, all we did was have a class on becoming a Marine.

They taught us that after we're Marines, there are restrictions on the civilian clothing we can wear when we're off-duty. We're still expected to be squared away, and we're not allowed to wear plain white T-shirts or ones with nasty trash printed on them. No problem. This recruit has learned how to be neat and clean, and maintain his military bearing, and he does not intend to backslide.

Now, it's time to go practice some rifle movements in the measly 30 minutes of free time I've got left. Only five days and a bowl of cereal to go.

Wearing my dogtags for the first time gave me a tremendous sense of pride of belonging. They also reminded me that very soon, I was going to be an official United States Marine.

SATURDAY, MAY 27: TD-53

Drill competition didn't go so well. We only managed third place, but our DIs handled it surprisingly well. I thought they'd be flipping out. I guess Marines don't cry over spilled milk. SDI Bixby even let us watch "A Few Good Men" while we cleaned our rifles. I sat near him during the movie. "Will we ever look at a military movie the same way again?" I whispered to SDI Bixby.

He shook his head, smiled and whispered, "Not a chance."

It was the first time I had ever heard him whisper. I didn't know he knew how! He's going to let us watch "Sniper" next – it's friggin' double-feature night here at First Battalion Squadbay Theatre. All of a sudden, life has become a lot easier. I even saw DI Parks laughing like a kid today. It was cool to see him in something other than his menacing form.

I got a special letter from Kimball at mail call. He sent me a specially modified quote from Shakespeare's Henry V that is totally awesome. I plan to share it with the platoon.

I put my dog tags on tonight for the first time, and it felt right. In a funny way, I'll be sad to leave Parris Island, but not all that sad. We're very close to leaving, but somehow, there's this feeling we'll never *really* leave.

There are only five freakin' days left, and we can all feel it – but it's like there is Novocain numbing the feeling. A chapter of my life is slowly coming to a close. Parris Island has given me rewards beyond my wildest dreams. Making the transition from boy to man is something I've been waiting for, for a long, LONG time. Now I can feel it. It's almost here.

SUNDAY, MAY 28

I just finished fire watch duty. Recruit Reilly and I bounced around like we owned the place. Reilly used the "contraband" camera Kimball sent me and took a picture of me in my cammies, posing in front of my rack, holding my rifle and with my dog tags hanging out (see next page). Sure hope it comes out. The recruit in the rack next to me saw the flash and didn't know what the hell was going on. Time to hit the rack.

It's now 0940 and we just got back from church. God day number 12 of 12. After a week-long deluge of recruits asking SDI Bixby to go to church with us, he finally gave in — so the whole friggin platoon went to church today. During the service, I stood at the front of the church and read the modified passage Kimball had sent me:

> Men forget; one day all shall be forgotten,
> But those among us will always remember the feats they did here.
> And when men toast the valiant, then shall our names — familiar in
>   their mouths as household words — be, in their flowing cups,
>   freshly remembered.
> Belleau Wood, Inchon, Iwo Jima, Kuwait City — and Parris Island.
> Our story shall good men teach their sons.
> From this day to the ending of the world, we shall be, in this Corps,
>   remembered —
> We few, we happy few, we band of brothers;
> For he that sheds his blood with me shall be my brother.
> We began as boys — this day we become men;
> And others, now in their beds,
> will think themselves accursed that they were not here,
> and hold their manhoods cheap while any speaks that fought with us,
> and earned the right to call himself, this day, a **United States Marine.**
>
> — *Paraphrasing Shakespeare, Henry V, Act IV, Scene III*

Awesome, is it not? It brought everyone in the whole church to their feet. After the service, a lot of recruits thanked me, and told me how great it was.

They let us make phone calls tonight, and when I called my mother and told her how much I loved church she almost had a heart attack. She said, "I can't wait to meet the new you." She won't have much longer to wait. Only three days and a wake-up to go!

MONDAY, MAY 29: TD-54

Just got back from chow. I took a motivational dump, then fell out with the platoon to take the final PFT (Physical Fitness Test). I had hoped that I'd be able to better, or at least equal, my previous best scores, which were 14 pull-ups, 84 sit-ups, and running 3 miles in 20 minutes and 45 seconds. The only thing that had me worried was the pull-ups.

And, as I feared, I was not able to equal my best pull-up score. I scored 13 pull-ups, 84 sit-ups, and ran 3 miles in 20:45. Not as good as I had hoped, but considering I ranked in the top third of the series, it's still an achievement.

Recruits Hockenberry and DeAngelis made it through, and as a platoon we did win the PFT once again. The series flag is ours all the way now. OOH-RAH! SDI Bixby is happy with our performance, because he says it will carry significant weight for him when it comes to promotions. As a reward for winning PFT, SDI Bixby let us watch another movie – "Menace II Society."

"Will we be getting a pizza party too?" we asked SDI Bixby.

"BLOW ME!" he shot back.

We all laughed.

We also had Esprit de Corps testing today. It was hard, but I think the DIs who gave the test had secret instructions to make everyone pass. I figure the paperwork they'd have to do if someone failed gives them great motivation to pass us all.

Everyone is chilling out right now, prepping for Battalion Commander's Inspection. We're almost unthinkably relaxed. I just took a ten-minute dump. Recruit Kuyher was in the head for so long, he fell asleep on the bowl. Even DI Parks, the Marine Machine, is sleeping in his chair. We just got our pictures back – the ones where we're wearing dress-blues. I can hardly believe it's me in that photo. I look mature, serious and proud. I look like a real Marine! It's hard to believe that soon I will actually be one. The chalkboard in the squad bay says, "4 days/11 chows to graduation! OOH-RAH!"

TUESDAY, MAY 30: TD-55

SDI Bixby told us at wake-up this morning, "IT AIN'T OVER UNTIL THE FAT LADY SINGS, BUT THAT OLD BITCH IS DONE GARGLING WATER AND PREPPING HER THROAT!"

Battalion Commander's Inspection went smooth as silk. By this point, we we're all finely tuned machines. Now the hard part was remembering how to talk.

"WHAT INFANTRY JOB DO YOU WANT, RECRUIT PRICE?"

I didn't know. I was so worried about graduating and becoming a Marine; I had forgotten all the snot nosed requests I made of my recruiter. However, now the time to start thinking of my future as a Marine was here. Off the top of my head I answered, "Sir, machine gunner, Sir."

"WHAT WAS THE BEST PART OF TRAINING?"

 "Sir, learning to get along with all the diverse personalities in the platoon, Sir."

"TEAMWORK!"

"SIR, YES, SIR!"

Recruit Barnes was the only problem – his rifle was STILL a mess. As punishment, he had to spend the entire day PTing and skuzzing the deck. I asked him how he felt, and he told me, "I'm mad at myself for letting down the platoon."

This morning we were feeling cocky, so we decided to aggravate DI Parks. He hates it when we say his name – it makes him crazy. So, when he gave us an order, we all yelled at once, "Aye, aye, Sergeant Parks, sir!"

He was taken aback, but when he realized we were doing it on purpose to aggravate him, he had to laugh. He pretended to strangle two recruits. We have a joke planned for each of our DIs every morning until graduation.

Now we're prepping our recruit liberty and graduation uniforms. Only one more day and a wake-up to go. Look out world... I'm coming home a United States Marine!

WEDNESDAY, MAY 31: TD-56

This morning's little joke on SDI Bixby didn't go so well – we had planned to get up before lights, put on our trench coats and boots, then get back in our racks and bust out when the lights went on. Bixby realized what was going on too soon, though, and stopped that trash in a heartbeat.

However, he didn't realize that we had a back-up plan. During breakfast, we all started chanting his name, pointing to him and singing, "Whoop, there he is! Whoop, there he is!"

After mess, we went to cash our checks and pay our final bills. My check was for $1,332, but after deducting the $132 on my debit card, plus the cost of all the stuff I ordered – yearbooks, photos, a ring and my plane ticket to SOI (School Of Infantry) – I was left with $900. We had outdoor graduation practice from around 1500 to 1700. For months, we've been waiting to conduct graduation practice, and now that it was finally here, all we wanted to do was the real thing. Our DIs are in high spirits. They're joking around with us more and more.

Another sign we've come full circle – all the documents we filled out that first night in receiving were returned to us, along with the civvies we wore coming in. DI Wight made us put them on. That was a flashback! Personally, I was disgusted with what I wore: a dirty, wrinkled Grateful Dead T-shirt and ripped-up jeans. These had been my favorite clothes?! I couldn't believe I actually used to dress like that. Never again. I couldn't wait to get that trash off and get back into my cammies. I didn't feel right again until I got them on.

Later we got our final Parris Island haircuts – the second high-and-tight. When the barber was done, I got out of the chair and saw myself in the mirror. It looked awesome. I couldn't believe I had ever looked any other way. That wasn't me. *This* was me. I'm starting to feel like a real Marine, and now I almost look like one too.

Wouldn't you know it? I pulled fire watch tonight – just like Private Joker in "Full Metal Jacket." Hope I don't find any Private Pyles in the head, ready to go bezerko. Tomorrow is Recruit Liberty. Finally, after 12 weeks, I get to see the people I love the most in the world. I wonder what they'll think when they see the new me.

THURSDAY, JUNE 1: TD-57

This morning's joke got SDI Bixby good. Right before lights, we all snuck over to his house (office) and started banging the crap out of his door. We scared the hell out of him. Platoon 1086 stacked all their mattresses against their DI's hatch. By 0430, he was borrowing our hose for some early morning "clean-up." Tomorrow, we will hit DI Ojeda with the mattress treatment.

We got pumped up with a five-mile motivational run around the Battalion areas, singing cadences loud as hell and ringing the battalion area bells. It seemed like the whole Island came alive to cheer us on. Afterward, the Commanding General himself spoke with us all. He looks like a kindly old man, but when he spoke, he really shook the house. He *was* a Marine, after all. He congratulated us each on earning the right to be called a Marine, and told us it's something we need to *keep on* earning every day. Exactly what Recruit Price intends to do. Then we quickly hurried to graduation practice – another hour of boredom. Today was hot and humid – REAL hot and humid. Recruit Jones almost passed out because he locked his knees and didn't drink enough water.

After that it was time to put on our Service Charlies – the uniform we'd wear to greet our families. When I saw myself in the mirror, it felt really great. All I could think of when I saw myself was, "This is good – REAL good. The USMC is gonna be one hell of a ride." We stepped outside for the pinning of the emblem ceremony, where we got the USMC globe and anchor pinned on our covers. It was short and sweet, but very meaningful because it represented the torch being passed to a new group of Marines. The ball is now in our court, just as the emblem is now on our covers.

Next, it was off to the Visitor's Center to meet my Mom, Dad, and brother, John, and my best friend, Kimball. When my Mother saw me, she ran over and kissed me. Being careful to maintain my military bearing, I hugged her back.

"Oh, my God," she said, "Billy, you've lost so much weight! You look like you're 16 again."

It was weird to hear someone calling me by my first name again. My father and brother shook my hand and congratulated me – Kimball just sort of stayed in the background. I wanted to bust out with a grin, but I was not about to lose my bearing. I flexed to him, and he shot me a satisfied glance. I knew he'd have something to say to me later in private. Plus, I could tell he was enjoying watching the proud expressions on my family's faces. From that point on, I began to realize how much I'd changed. My whole attitude is different now – I'm no longer a cocky, obnoxious kid – I'm a man, full of confidence. I escorted them around Parris Island, showing them the Confidence course, acting like I was the Depot Commander himself.

"Will," my brother told me, "The way you're walking is different. You walk like... "

"...a Marine," my father finished, "I'm *very* proud of you, son."

During my little "tour," my family lagged behind at one point and I walked alone next to Kimball. He had something to tell me.

"Will, the changes in you are really amazing. You look absolutely fantastic – but there's much more to it than that. You seem so confident, like you finally know who you are. You're different inside. You've got an inner core of seriousness that was never there before. You've done it, Price. You've finally grown up, and I'm so proud of you."

"Thank you, sir!" I told him, "I've been waiting a long time to show you."

He smiled, and I know we were both remembering that night in the Marine Recruiter's office a lifetime ago. With all my heart, I truly felt proud. It was one of the greatest days in my life.

FRIDAY, JUNE 2 - GRADUATION DAY

"THREE MINUTES TO LIGHTS!"

"TWO MINUTES TO LIGHTS!"

"ONE MINUTE TO LIGHTS!"

O-Dark Thirty or 0330. The lights went on as usual. However, today was special – TD-58 was finally here. We got an early start on folding our linen and getting it properly turned in. Just after 0500, we marched off to our last chow as a platoon on Parris Island. Business as usual – but it all felt strangely sad, knowing we, Platoon 1082, would not ever return to that chow hall.

After breakfast, we had our last squad bay field day, then proceeded to

Graduation Day for Recruit Price. I finally feel like a real Marine.

don our graduation uniforms. Suddenly all the blood, sweat, and tears we had invested in Boot Camp began turning into feelings of uncontrollable happiness. This feeling just grew and grew as we had our final graduation practice, then returned to our First Battalion home and used our final hour to say good-bye. SDI Bixby gave us a very moving speech that almost brought everyone to tears. He even looked like he was tearing up himself. Imagine that! SDI Bixby really *is* human after all.

SDI Bixby and DI Parks then conducted a little ceremony where they awarded Recruits Lish, Hillman and Tran meritorious promotions to Private First Class. Surrounded by the platoon, they received their promotions, as well as a punch on the arm from each of our DIs. Then, the time had come. The parade deck – and graduation – waited. We marched out, sharper and prouder than life, repeating after SDI Bixby, as he chanted:

YOU CAN KEEP YOUR ARMY KHAKI,
YOU CAN KEEP YOUR NAVY BLUE,
I HAVE THE WORLD'S BEST FIGHTING MAN,
TO INTRODUCE TO YOU,

HIS UNIFORM IS DIFFERENT,
THE BEST YOU'VE EVER SEEN,
THE GERMANS CALL HIM "DEVIL DOG,"
HIS REAL NAME IS MARINE!

HE WAS BORN ON PARRIS ISLAND,
THE LAND THAT GOD FORGOT,
THE SAND IS EIGHTEEN INCHES DEEP,
THE SUN IS MIGHTY HOT.

HE GETS UP EVERY MORNING
BEFORE THE RISING SUN
HE'LL RUN A HUNDRED MILES
BEFORE THE DAY IS DONE

HE'S DEADLY WITH A RIFLE
A BAYONET MADE OF STEEL
HE TOOK THE WARRIOR'S CALLING CARD
HE'S MASTERED HOW TO KILL

Platoon 1082 finally gets their day on the parade deck as the boys from Company C go marching tall in our Dress Blue Delta uniforms, the same ones I had admired just four months ago in my recruiter's office.

AND WHEN HE GETS TO HEAVEN
ST. PETER HE WILL TELL
"ONE MORE MARINE REPORTING, SIR
I'VE SERVED MY TIME IN HELL."

SO LISTEN ALL YOU YOUNG GIRLS
TO WHAT I HAVE TO SAY
GO FIND YOURSELF A YOUNG MARINE
TO LOVE YOU EVERY DAY

HE'LL HUG YOU AND HE'LL KISS YOU
AND TREAT YOU LIKE A QUEEN
THERE IS NO BETTER FIGHTING MAN
THE UNITED STATES MARINE!

We assumed our position near the parade deck. In the distant bleachers, we could see our families and friends waiting to watch us graduate and become Marines. As the band that preceded us, marched onto the parade deck, I marveled at their skill and precision. "Even Marine band members," I thought to myself, "are the elite." In just a minute, this amazing brotherhood was about to welcome me to its ranks. It would all be me.

We marched onto the parade deck in perfect unison. When we finally halted, we assumed parade rest position, then the position of attention, while we listened to a number of speeches. They lasted about half an hour, during which time we all stood perfectly still in the blistering 90 degree heat. "This is nothing," I thought. "I've stood still for way longer."

"YOU'RE STANDING HERE TODAY," our commander's voice boomed over the loud speaker, "IN YOUR CRISP, NEW UNIFORMS. YOUR SHOES, YOUR BRASS – THEY GLEAM JUST LIKE MIRRORS. YOU LOOK SHARP! BUT ALWAYS REMEMBER... UNTIL THE DAY THAT YOU DIE, DEEP INSIDE EACH AND EVERYONE OF YOU THERE HAS BEEN BORN AND BRED AN INDIVIDUAL WHO WILL ALWAYS BE THAT DIRTY, SWEATY, FILTH-ENCRUSTED, RIPPED-TROUSERED, CAMOUFLAGE-PAINTED, MAGNIFICENT LITTLE SON OF A GUN WHOSE BRETHREN HAVE KEPT THE WOLF AWAY FROM THE DOOR OF THIS NATION FOR OVER 220 YEARS. GO FORTH AS **MARINES**, AND JOIN YOUR BRETHREN IN THAT WATCH."

Now it was time for THE moment.

"SENIOR DRILL INSTRUCTORS – DISMISS YOUR PLATOONS!"

SDI Bixby sounded off. "PLATOON ONE THOUSAND EIGHTY-TWO... DISMISSED!!!"

We roared back with a single voice, loud enough to tear a hole in the sky.

"DISMISSED, AYE SIR!!!"

The band began to play, and our families rushed out onto the deck to congratulate us. We had done it. We were no longer recruits. WE WERE UNITED STATES MARINES!

It was a great feeling to congratulate my fellow Marines – still, I did not go overboard. That military bearing trash really does become a part of you. As I shook SDI Staff Sgt. Bixby's hand, he looked a little uncomfortable about the mob of families rushing toward us. There was no telling them, "GET THE HELL AWAY FROM ME BEFORE I MAKE YOUR STINKIN' HEAD EXPLODE." I could tell he did not like the idea of being approached by so many civilians.

DI Staff Sgt. Wight did not delay his escape either. He made a quick exit, and I didn't get to say good-bye to him. I can't say it really bothered me. DI Staff Sgt. Ojeda was too far away by the time my family neared, and so I didn't get to say good-bye to him either. We had spoken earlier, so I'll consider that my good-bye to him. I didn't know where DI Sgt. Parks was.

Not a Marine among us had gone unchanged by the last twelve weeks. There were some that, like fighting the effects of hypnotism, resisted Boot Camp – and so all they got out of it was an improved physique. They had not learned all they could about discipline, respect, pride, the Corps – or themselves. But most of 1082 had come through the experience transformed.

Speaking for myself, I had learned more in the last three months, than I ever learned in my whole life. Physically, mentally, and spiritually, I am light years ahead. For years, I had been searching for the meaning of life without finding anything. The Marines finally opened the "hatch" for me. Like someone once told me, the Marines are my "lever," and now I'm ready to move the world!

I thank you, Parris Island, for kicking my tail up and down, teaching me, and guiding me to the light. "We began as boys, this day we become men." I feel extremely lucky that I've been given another chance at life through the grace of the United States Marine Corps. All the mistakes I made prior to joining up have now been erased. Like the Phoenix, I've risen from the ashes to soar once more.

Within me, I feel a burning sense of pride. It's in my walk, it's in my talk, and it's here to stay. It's in me for good – it IS me. My eyes have a greater sense of focus, my ears pick up more, my arms and legs are stronger – my entire persona has been sculpted and sharpened and motivated. And there's no way in hell I'm ever going back. I've seen how good life can be when you have respect, confidence and inner peace. These attributes are priceless.

What I've experienced was the transformation of an unhappy and confused boy with no future into a full-fledged man – a Marine – with a deep sense of self and inner pride. I thank my mother, father, brother, my best friend, and the whole United States Marine Corps for seeing to it that PFC. Price became a United States Marine.

On the day before Graduation, you get to spend time with your family and friends. Pictured here is my dad, Bill Sr., brother John, and my mother Carolyn. I love this picture, because my Mom looks like she's amazed by the changes in me. Hi Mom!

Less than a year after stepping on those yellow footprints, here is Lance Cpl. Price after an all-night vehicle patrol in Guantanamo Bay, Cuba, as a United States Marine. I couldn't ask for anything better.

THE FLEET

Back home on ten days leave, it wasn't long before I realized again how much I'd changed. I still got up every morning at 0500, and tried to fill each day with activity. Monday, I went to visit some friends and teachers from my old high school and everybody was all over me – it was like I'd just come back from a war. I was a hero.

Tuesday, I hit the beach with Kimball. He told me that I was a man now, and that the career I had chosen was a very fulfilling one, but dangerous too. He said "You may get hurt, you may even *die*, but you will never regret the choice you've made. And neither will I. As Shakespeare (him again) said, 'Cowards die a million times before their death, the valiant taste of death but once.'"

Tuesday, I went to a Yankee ballgame with my friends. I was a little bit disgusted at the way they had no discipline at all, and no goals. I saw them a whole different way. I've changed – I'll never look at anything the same way again.

Wednesday, it was volleyball in the back yard with my brother John and his friends. Thursday, I had a bar-b-que, and Friday I cleaned my room and went out with Jenifer to a movie. On Saturday, I started thinking about reporting to the next phase of my training – SOI (School of Infantry) in Camp LeJuene, North Carolina.

I noticed my hair was getting long. It had been more than a week since my last high-and-tight, and it was time for another. No one had to tell me to get a haircut, I just wanted one. There was no way I was showing up for Infantry training looking like a hippie. Not this Marine. After getting a haircut, I went home and spent the rest of the day ironing my uniforms and packing my seabag. Sunday was spent with my father in Manhattan, then on Monday morning, at 0500, it was off to the airport.

I'm writing this on a flight to North Carolina, ending this diary the way I began it – on a plane flight. But what a difference in the writer. Now, I know who I am. Remember those dirty, sweaty, filth-encrusted, ripped-trousered, camouflage-painted, magnificent little son of a guns who've kept the wolf away from the door of this nation for over 220 years? I'm one of them now. They call us *Marines*.

DEVIL DOG GLOSSARY

ABOARD: On base, with us

ALL HANDS: Every member of a command

AS YOU WERE: Resume what you were doing, make a correction

BCD: Bad Conduct Discharge

BCG: Birth Control Goggles, or military-issued glasses

BARRACKS COVER: Garrison (frame) hat

BELAY: Stop something, cease activity

BELAY THAT: Cancel or disregard previous statement or order

BILLET: Assignment, job, place of residence

BIVOUAC: A camp in the field

BLOUSE: Uniform jacket ("Tuck in or your blouse, secure your blouse.")

BLOUSING BANDS: Elastic bands used to secure utility trouser cuffs

BLUES: Marine Dress Blue uniform

BOOT: Recruit, training Marine, new Marine

BRAIN HOUSING GROUP: Brain, head

BRASS: Officers

BRIG: Jail

BROWN BAGGER: A married Marine who brings lunch to work

BULKHEAD: Wall

BUTTERBAR: A second Lieutenant (refers to gold rank insignia bar)

BY THE NUMBERS: Perform methodically, following official sequence

CG: Commanding General

CO: Commanding Officer

CP: Command Post in the field

CARRY ON: Resume what you were doing

CHIT: Written authorization, receipt

CHOW: Food

CHOW HALL: Dining hall

CLICK: One notch of adjustment on a rifle (A "klick" is a kilometer)

COLORS: Flag

CORPSMAN: A Navy medic serving with the Marines

COVER: Hat

CONUS: Continental United States

CW-1,2,3,4: Levels of swim qualification

DECK: Floor

DIDDY BAG: Cloth bag for small items

DIDDY BOP: Swagger, affected walk

DOG-AND-PONY-SHOW: Small presentation, minor event

DOUBLE TIME: Quickly

DRY RUN: Practice

EL MARKO: Magic marker

ENTRENCHING TOOL (E-TOOL): Small field shovel

FARTSACK: Mattress cover

FIELD STRIP: Disassemble; take apart

FIRE IN THE HOLE: Warning that explosives are about to be detonated

FLEET: Fleet Marine Force

FMF: Fleet Marine Force

GALLEY: Kitchen

GANG WAY: Stand back, move away

GEE-DUNK: Candy, soda, junk food

GEAR: Equipment

GET SOME: Engage the enemy, get a piece of the action

GI CAN: Garbage can

GO FASTERS: Running sneakers

GRAPE: A person's head

GRINDER: Parade ground

GUIDON: Flag showing unit designation

GUNG HO: Chinese term meaning literally "work together," also: highly motivated.

GUNNY: Gunnery Sergeant
GRAB ASS, ORGANIZED
GRAB-ASS: Play, sport,
  frivolous activity
GREEN MACHINE: The U.S.
  Marine Corps

HARD CHARGER: A highly
  enthusiastic Marine or recruit
HATCH: Door
HEAD: Toilet, bathroom
HEAVY: The DI who disciplines
recruits the hardest
HIGH-AND-TIGHT: Standard
  Marine haircut, shaved sides
  and short on top
HOLLYWOOD MARINE:
  Attended boot camp in
  San Diego
HOOCH: Any kind of shelter,
  residence
HOUSE MOUSE: Drill
  Instructor's assistant
HUMP: March, carry, be burdened
  with

INCOMING: Hostile fire being
received
INK STICK: Pen
IRISH PENNANTS: Threads
  dangling from clothing
  indicating unkempt appearance
IPT: Incentive Physical Training
ITR: Infantry Training Regiment

JARHEAD: Marine (refers to the
  jar and lid like appearance of
  high and tight haircut)
JIBS: Teeth ("I'll bust your jibs!")
JUNK-ON-THE-BUNK: Full
  clothing and equipment
  inspection
K-BAR: Marine-issued fighting
  knife
KLICK: Kilometer

LADDER WELL: Stairs
LEAVE: Time off of more than 24
  hours
LIBERTY: Time off of less than
  24 hours

L.I.N.E. training: Linear
  Infighting Neurological
  Override Engagement training
LOCK AND LOAD: Arm and
ready your weapon, get ready

MAKE A HOLE: Stand back,
  gangway
MAGGIE'S DRAWERS: Red disc
  used on the rifle range, signifies
  a missed target
MCMAP: Marine Corps Martial
  Arts Program
MOON BEAM: Flashlight
MOS: Marine Occupational
  Specialty, your assigned job
  position
MUSTANG (MUSTANGER):
  Enlisted man who becomes
  an officer

OFFICE POGUE: Desk-bound
  Marine
OVERHEAD: Ceiling
OVER THE HILL: Absent
  without authorization

PASSAGEWAY: Corridor;
  hallway
PIECE: Rifle
PISS CUTTER: Type of hat,
  envelope-shaped overseas cap
POGUE: Lazy individual or office
  worker
POGEY BAIT: Candy, sweets
POLICE CALL: Clean up an area
POP-UP FLARE: Hand held
  aerial illumination flare
PT: Physical Training, exercise

QUARTERS: living space
QUARTERDECK: Area outside
  DI's office, typically used
  for IPT

RACK: Bed, bunk
RAPPEL: To descend from cliff
  or helicopter by rope
RECON, FORCE RECON: A
  Force Reconnaissance Marine
ROMP 'N' STOMP: drill, march

ROUND: Bullet, artillery or
mortar shell

SALT: Experience
SALTY: Experienced, smart
mouthed;
SCRIBE: Recruit who acts as a
DI's secretary
SCUTTLEBUTT: Rumor; a
drinking fountain
SEABAG: Duffle bag
SEA DUTY: Tour aboard a ship
SEA STORY: Lie, exaggeration
SEA LAWYER: Self-appointed
expert
SECURE: Tie down, make fast,
recycle/dispose of; put
something in its place;
cease and desist
SEVEN-EIGHTY-TWO GEAR:
Field equipment, canvas
web gear
SHIT BIRD: Messy or
undisciplined person,
a chronic screw-up
SHIT CAN: Garbage can
SHORT: Nearing the end of a
tour of duty or enlistment
SHORT TIMER: Marine or
recruit nearing the end of
a tour
SHORT ROUND: Ordnance
that lands away from a target
SICK BAY: Clinic or hospital
SKIPPER: Captain,
commanding officer
SKIVVIES: Underwear
SKUZZ BRUSH: Foot long
brush to sweep squad bay
SMOKING LAMP: Authority to
smoke (when this light is lit)
SNAP IN: Practice firing
techniques with rifle
SNOOPIN' AND POOPIN':
Reconnoiter, search for
indiscreetly
SNOT LOCKER: Nose
SOUND OFF: Yell loudly
SONARS: Ears
SQUAD BAY: Barracks
SQUARED AWAY: Neat, orderly,

organized.
SQUID: A sailor
STACK ARMS: Place three or
more rifles in a pyramid
STACKING SWIVEL:
Appendage near muzzle of
rifle allowing stacked arms;
neck
STAND BY: Prepare, wait
STANDBY: Waiting status
SWAB: Mop
SWABBIE: Sailor

TOPSIDE: Upstairs; on deck
TURN TO: Begin work

UA: Unauthorized Absence
UNQ: Unqualified, Marine who
fails to qualifying at the
rifle range

WORD, THE WORD:
Confirmed official
information; the straight
scoop (as opposed to gossip
or hearsay)

ZERO-DARK-THIRTY: Pre
dawn; early

A B O U T   T H E   A U T H O R

WILLIAM PRICE was born in the Bronx, New York, in 1971. He graduated from Gorton High School in Yonkers, Albany State University in Albany, New York, and from Marine Boot Camp on Parris Island as a Private First Class. After becoming a Marine, the author/infantryman was stationed in Guantanamo Bay, Cuba, for a year. This service was followed by two successive tours of duty in the Mediterranean Sea, while stationed at Camp LeJeune, North Carolina. After this, Sgt. Price became the Press Chief at Marine Corps Air Station Beaufort, South Carolina. The author next became the Marketing and Public Affairs Representative for Marine Recruiting Station Jacksonville, Florida. The former Recruit Price, now Gunnery Sgt. Will Price, is currently the Public Affairs Chief of Marine Barracks, Washington, D.C., "The Oldest Post In The Corps."

A C K N O W L E D G E M E N T S

Thanks to Kirk Kimball for encouraging me to make the best decision of my life, to become a United States Marine. Thanks also to my recruiter, Staff Sgt. Snyder, and all my drill instructors, for sticking with me and helping to mold me into one of the Few and the Proud. I also want to thank Dr. Cal Atwood, Jenifer Jones, Staff Sgt. Bryce Piper, Sgt. Reina Barnett, Danielle Cooley, Cpl. David Revere, Chris Noel, Dr. Susan Shaw, William Landon Price, and my uncle, LCpl. Bob Price, USMC. Thanks also to my son Will Price III, my brother John, my father William, and special thanks to my mother, Carolyn.

Price in Afghanistan